CAMBRIDGE
UNIVERSITY PRESS

Biology

for Cambridge IGCSE™

ENGLISH LANGUAGE SKILLS WORKBOOK

Matthew Broderick & Timothy Chadwick

CAMBRIDGE
UNIVERSITY PRESS

University Printing House, Cambridge CB2 8BS, United Kingdom

One Liberty Plaza, 20th Floor, New York, NY 10006, USA

477 Williamstown Road, Port Melbourne, VIC 3207, Australia

314–321, 3rd Floor, Plot 3, Splendor Forum, Jasola District Centre, New Delhi – 110025, India

103 Penang Road, #05–06/07, Visioncrest Commercial, Singapore 238467

Cambridge University Press is part of the University of Cambridge.

It furthers the University's mission by disseminating knowledge in the pursuit of education, learning and research at the highest international levels of excellence.

www.cambridge.org
Information on this title: www.cambridge.org/9781108947503

© Cambridge University Press 2022

First edition 2022

20 19 18 17 16 15 14 13 12 11 10 9 8 7 6 5 4 3 2 1

Printed in Italy by L.E.G.O. S.p.A.

A catalogue record for this publication is available from the British Library

ISBN 978-1-108-94750-3 English Language Skills Workbook with Digital Access (2 Years)

Additional resources for this publication at www.cambridge.org/go

Illustrations by Eleanor Jones

We would like to thank Fiona Mauchline and Sally Burbeary for their valuable contributions to this book.

DEDICATED TEACHER AWARDS

Teachers play an important part in shaping futures. Our Dedicated Teacher Awards recognise the hard work that teachers put in every day.

Thank you to everyone who nominated this year; we have been inspired and moved by all of your stories. Well done to all of our nominees for your dedication to learning and for inspiring the next generation of thinkers, leaders and innovators.

Congratulations to our incredible winners!

WINNER

Regional Winner Middle East & North Africa	Regional Winner Europe	Regional Winner North & South America	Regional Winner Central & Southern Africa	Regional Winner Australia, New Zealand & South-East Asia	Regional Winner East & South Asia
Annamma Lucy GEMS Our Own English High School, Sharjah - Boys' Branch, UAE	Anna Murray British Council, France	Melissa Crosby Frankfort High School, USA	Nonhlanhla Masina African School for Excellence, South Africa	Peggy Pesik Sekolah Buin Batu, Indonesia	Raminder Kaur Mac Choithram School, India

For more information about our dedicated teachers and their stories, go to
dedicatedteacher.cambridge.org

CAMBRIDGE
UNIVERSITY PRESS

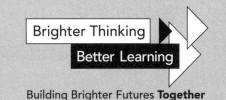

Brighter Thinking
Better Learning

Building Brighter Futures **Together**

> Contents

> How to use this series

We offer a comprehensive, flexible array of resources for the Cambridge IGCSE™ Biology syllabus. We provide targeted support and practice for the specific challenges we've heard that students face: learning science with English as a second language; learners who find the mathematical content within science difficult; and developing practical skills.

The coursebook provides coverage of the full Cambridge IGCSE Biology syllabus. Each chapter explains facts and concepts, and uses relevant real-world examples of scientific principles to bring the subject to life. Together with a focus on practical work and plenty of active learning opportunities, the coursebook prepares learners for all aspects of their scientific study. At the end of each chapter, examination-style questions offer practice opportunities for learners to apply their learning.

The digital teacher's resource contains detailed guidance for all topics of the syllabus, including common misconceptions identifying areas where learners might need extra support, as well as an engaging bank of lesson ideas for each syllabus topic. Differentiation is emphasised with advice for identification of different learner needs and suggestions of appropriate interventions to support and stretch learners. The teacher's resource also contains support for preparing and carrying out all the investigations in the practical workbook, including a set of sample results for when practicals aren't possible.

The teacher's resource also contains scaffolded worksheets and unit tests for each chapter. Answers for all components are accessible to teachers for free on the Cambridge GO platform.

The skills-focused workbook has been carefully constructed to help learners develop the skills that they need as they progress through their Cambridge IGCSE Biology course, providing further practice of all the topics in the coursebook. A three-tier, scaffolded approach to skills development enables students to gradually progress through 'focus', 'practice' and 'challenge' exercises, ensuring that every learner is supported. The workbook enables independent learning and is ideal for use in class or as homework.

The practical workbook provides learners with additional opportunities for hands-on practical work, giving them full guidance and support that will help them to develop their investigative skills. These skills include planning investigations, selecting and handling apparatus, creating hypotheses, recording and displaying results, and analysing and evaluating data.

Mathematics is an integral part of scientific study, and one that learners often find a barrier to progression in science. The Maths Skills for Cambridge IGCSE Biology write-in workbook has been written in collaboration with the Association for Science Education, with each chapter focusing on several maths skills that students need to succeed in their Biology course.

Our research shows that English language skills are the single biggest barrier to students accessing international science. This write-in English language skills workbook contains exercises set within the context of Cambridge IGCSE Biology topics to consolidate understanding and embed practice in aspects of language central to the subject. Activities range from practising using 'effect' and 'affect' in the context of enzymes, to writing about expiration with a focus on common prefixes.

> How to use this book

Throughout this book, you will notice lots of different features that will help your learning. These are explained below.

INTRODUCTION

This sets the scene for each chapter.

LEARNING INTENTIONS

These set out the learning intentions for each exercise. Each exercise will help you to develop both your English skills and your Biology skills.

KEY WORDS

Key vocabulary and definitions are given in boxes at the start of exercises. You will also find definitions of these words in the Glossary at the back of this book.

Exercises

These help you to develop and practise your English skills alongside your Biology skills.

LANGUAGE FOCUS

These give you more information about parts of the English language that you may find challenging, to help you use English more fluently.

LANGUAGE TIP

The information in these boxes will help you complete the questions using correct English, and give you support in areas that you might find difficult.

These boxes tell you where information in the book is extension content, and is not part of the syllabus.

> Supplement content

Where content is intended for students who are studying the Supplement content of the syllabus as well as the Core, this is indicated with the arrow and bar, as you can see on the left here.

> Introduction

Welcome to this workbook, which will help you with your study of Biology using English. To progress well in your studies in Biology, it will help if you can also use the English language well in a way that is appropriate to science. If you can read English well, you can understand what is written in your Biology textbook easily. If you can write and speak English well, you can share your knowledge about Biology with others easily.

This workbook will help you understand some important topics in Biology. It will also help you develop your skills in English. The exercises will give you practice in both things at the same time.

The exercises will help your English skills in different ways. They will:

*   help you understand the meaning of important words

*   help you to use certain types of words correctly, like nouns and adjectives

*   help you to construct sentences correctly

*   help you to construct whole passages of text

*   give you practice in reading text and extracting information from it.

The areas of English covered in this book have been chosen because they are useful to understand and discuss the subject of Biology. Aspects of language are discussed directly to help you understand certain exercises, and to explain why these aspects are useful to you as you learn Biology. You will be able to link these explanations to the content of your English language course.

We hope you enjoy using this book, and that you progress well in your studies of Biology and English.

Note for teachers:

Additional teaching ideas for this English Language Skills Workbook are available on Cambridge GO, downloadable with this workbook and the Cambridge IGCSE Biology Teacher's Resource. This includes engaging activities to use in lessons, with guidance on differentiation and assessment.

Answers to all questions in this English Language Skills Workbook are also accessible to teachers at www.cambridge.org/go

> Skills grid

Chapter	Exercises	Main language topics
1 Characteristics and classification of living organisms	Characteristics of living organisms Constructing a key Describing organisms Kingdom to species	The present simple tense
2 Cells	The parts of a cell Comparing cells Organisation of cells	Describing differences using *but* and *however* Describing similarities using *both* Using *a* and *an*
3 Movement into and out of cells	Key words Describing diffusion Describing and explaining osmosis	Using *will* or *will not* with a verb, to express certainty Using command words
4 Biological molecules	Chemicals of life – vocabulary Sentences about carbohydrates Planning a food test	Using the prefixes *mono-*, *di-*, *tri-* and *poly-* for numbers Writing a report using the passive voice
5 Enzymes	Key words for enzymes Effect of temperature on enzymes Using enzymes in industry	Using scientific words to write more effectively Giving examples using *for example*, *such as*, *for instance* and *including*
6 Plant nutrition	Inorganic to organic Limiting factors Mineral ion deficiencies in plants Words to describe plants	Using the prefixes *in-* and *im-* Vocabulary for describing graphs Making conclusions using *therefore*, *consequently*, *so* or *which suggests* Using common English words in a scientific context
7 Human nutrition	Recommending a balanced diet Digestive enzymes Digestion key words The journey of digestion	Using *fewer*, *less* and *more* with countable and uncountable nouns Using the passive voice to talk about the present Understanding the difference between noun and verb forms of words
8 Transport in plants	Key words in plant transport Linking structure to function Explaining the effect of conditions on plants	Recognising key words in pieces of text Linking causes and effects using *so*, *consequently* and *because* Using the first conditional for predictions: *will*, *can*, *could*, *should*, *might* and *may*

Chapter	Exercises	Main language topics
9 Transport in animals	Oxygen in the blood Taking care of your heart Blood vessels Effect of exercise on heart rate	Using *this* to talk about things near to us (in space or time) Giving advice using *should*, *ought to* and *X is good for you* Using prepositions to talk about motion or direction Using the command words *describe* and *explain*
10 Diseases and immunity	Key words in diseases and immunity Cholera Immunity Army	The difference between *affect* and *effect* Making comparisons using *like*, *similar to* and *different to/from*
11 Respiration and gas exchange	Equations of respiration The importance of respiration Aerobic and anaerobic respiration Gas exchange in humans Breathing in and breathing out	Word families Using *while* and *whereas* to express contrast Making plurals
12 Coordination and response	Responding to stimuli Reflex arcs Nervous system versus endocrine system	Recognising and learning key words Adverbs of manner (descriptive adverbs), including *quickly*, *easily*, *hard*
13 Excretion and homeostasis	Key concepts in excretion and homeostasis Homeostasis The human excretory system	Expressing difference using *more than* or *less than* Writing explanations using *which* and *this* Changing passive sentences into active sentences
14 Reproduction in plants	Asexual and sexual reproduction Sexual reproduction in plants Types of pollination	Using linking words to express sequence: *first, then, next, after that, finally* Using linking words to express results: *as a result of this, this means, consequently*
15 Reproduction in humans	Human sex cells Puberty in males and females Fertilisation and implantation	Using the suffix *-ing* to describe what is happening Using words to describe change, including *start, eventually, gain, broaden* Using verb agreement correctly

Chapter	Exercises	Main language topics
16 Chromosomes, genes and proteins	Structure of a chromosome Mitosis and meiosis Dominant and recessive alleles Codominance and blood groups	Using prefixes to identify the meaning of a word Using modal verbs for certainty and possibility Expressing probability using *unlikely to*, *could*, *be likely to* and *should*
17 Variation and selection	Key words of variation Darwin and evolution Adaptation of a lion	The simple past tense Using *because*, *as*, *so that* and *in order that* to express purpose or reason
18 Organisms and their environment	Ecological key terms Food chains and food webs The human population	Hypothesising using the second conditional tense Vocabulary to describe increases and decreases (in numbers)
19 Human influences on ecosystems	Habitat destruction Endangered species Climate change Limiting the effects of climate change	Using the zero conditional to describe facts and known truths Meanings of the letter *s* when used at the end of a word Linking cause and effect using *due to*, *owing to*, *because of* and *(be) caused by* Using the second conditional to express hypothetical situations
20 Biotechnology and genetic modification	Key words Pectinase in fruit juice production Genetic modification	Using *a*, *an* and *the* correctly Review of the passive voice Using prepositions

> Skills and support

Introduction

This section includes information about English language skills which are essential for you in order understand science concepts and to communicate your science ideas effectively to others.

You can use this English reference section at any time to support your studies in science.

Quick reference guide

Grammar	Use	Example
noun (n)	A word to show the name of a person, place or object.	A *biologist*. A science *laboratory*. A *graph*.
verb (v)	A word to show an action or state.	I *investigate* the theory. Plants *need* water.
adjective (adj)	A word to describe the quality or state of a noun.	The *flexible* tube. The *strong* flow.

Verbs

Present simple

The present simple is used to talk about facts and things that are generally true. It can also be used to talk about habits and routines and often with verbs of senses and perception, for example: *think*, *hurt*, *understand*.

There are different groups of verbs in English, for example, the verb *to be*, regular verbs and irregular verbs.

The verb *to be* can be used to describe somebody or something and can be followed by adjectives and nouns.

	Positive	Negative	Question
I	am	am not	Am I...?
You	are	are not	Are you...?
He	is	is not	Is he...?
She	is	is	Is she...?
It	is	is not	Is it...?
We	are	are not	Are we...?
They	are	are not	Are they...?

Example sentences:

Affirmative	Negative	Question
I am a scientist.	I am not a scientist.	Am I a scientist?
It is a fish.	It is not a fish.	Is it a fish?
They are birds.	You are not a bird.	Are they birds?

Regular verbs in the present

With *I*, *you*, *we* and *they*, use the verb. For example, *I read, we go.*

With *he*, *she* and *it*, add -*s* or -*es* to the verb. For example, *he reads, it goes.*

	Affirmative	Negative	Question
I, you, we, they	+ verb	*do not* + verb	*Do* + pronoun / noun + verb?
he, she, it	+ verb + -s or -es	*does not* + verb	*Does* + pronoun / noun + verb?

With verbs ending in a consonant (b, c, d, f, g, etc.) + *y*, change the *y* to an *i* and then add -*es* when it follows *he*, *she*, *it*. For example, *you fly, it fli̲e̲s̲.*

When the verb ends in -*ch*, -*ss*, -*sh*, -*x* or -*zz* also add -*es* in the affirmative form when it follows *he*, *she*, *it*. For example, *she watches.*

With verbs ending in a vowel (a, e, i, o, u) + *y*, add -*s* when it follows *he*, *she*, *it*. For example, *I stay*, *he stay̲s̲.*

	Affirmative	Negative	Question
I, you, we, they	I eat fish.	I do not eat fish.	Do I eat fish?
	They swim in water.	They don't swim in water.	Do they swim in water?
	They live in nests.	They do not live in nests.	Do they live in nests?
he, she, it	She eats fish.	She does not eat fish.	Does she eat fish?
	It swims in water.	It doesn't swim in water.	Does it swim in water?
	It lives in a nest.	It does not live in a nest.	Does it live in a nest?

Irregular verbs in the present

	Affirmative	Negative	Question
I, you, we, they	I have wings.	I don't have wings.	Do I have wings?
	They go underwater.	They do not go underwater.	Do they go underwater?
	They do investigations.	They don't do investigations.	Do they do investigations?
he, she, it	It has a beak.	It doesn't have a beak.	Does it have a beak?
	He goes underwater.	He does not go underwater.	Does he go underwater?
	She does investigations.	She doesn't do investigations.	Does she do investigations?

Be careful with irregular plurals that are from Greek and Latin, make sure you know which is singular and which is plural. Be sure to use *is* with the singular and *are* with the plural form.

> An *alveolus* is a very small air sac at the end of the bronchioles. *Alveoli* are tiny air sacs of the lungs where rapid gaseous exchange takes place, during the process of breathing in and breathing out.

Past simple

The past simple is used to talk about finished past actions.

Remember the verb *to be* is used to describe somebody or something and is followed by names, ages, feelings and professions.

	Affirmative	Negative	Question
I	was	was not	Was I...?
You	were	were not	Were you...?
He	was	was not	Was he...?
She	was	was not	Was she...?
It	was	was not	Was it...?
We	were	were not	Were we...?
They	were	were not	Were they...?

Example sentences:

Affirmative	Negative	Question
I was a student.	I was not a student.	Was I a student?
It was a caterpillar.	It was not a caterpillar.	Was it a caterpillar?
They were eggs.	They were not eggs.	Were they eggs?

Regular verbs in the past simple

	Affirmative	Negative	Question
I, you, we, they, he, she, it	+ verb + -ed	*did not* + verb	*Did* + verb *to be* + verb?

With verbs ending in the letter *e*, just add *-d*. For example, *I observe, I observe<u>d</u>*.

With verbs ending in a consonant (b, c, d, f, g, etc.) + *y*, change the *y* to an *i* and then add *-ed* when it follows *he, she, it*. For example, *you try, you tr<u>ied</u>*.

	Affirmative	Negative	Question
I, you, he, she, it, we, they	I *observed* the changes.	I *did not observe* the changes.	*Did* I *observe* the changes?
	It *destroyed* the cells.	It *didn't destroy* the cells.	*Did* it *destroy* the cells?
	They *carried* oxygen.	They *didn't carry* oxygen.	*Did* they *carry* oxygen?

Irregular verbs in the past simple

	Affirmative	Negative	Question
I, you, he, she, it, we, they	It *became* heavy.	It *didn't become* heavy.	*Did* it *become* heavy?
	She *grew* quickly.	She *did not grow* quickly.	*Did* she *grow* quickly?
	They *shook* violently.	They *did not shake* violently.	*Did* they *shake* violently?

Verb + *ing*

When you want to describe something, you can use *when it is* + verb + *-ing* or *when they are* + verb + *-ing*.

> Sperm have tails. These help the sperm to move, *when it is swimming* towards the ovum (egg cell). →
> This helps the sperm, *when swimming* towards the ovum (egg cell).

The zero conditional

The zero conditional is used to talk about facts and things that are generally true. The structure is: *if/when* + present simple + present simple.

	Condition	Result
If	you heat ice,	it melts.
If	muscles become cold,	they shake.
If	animals do not eat,	they die.

It is possible to start with the results clause. Notice that if you start with the *if* clause, a comma is needed. If you start with the results clause, a comma is not needed.

> *If* you heat ice, it melts.
> Ice melts *if* you heat it.

The first conditional

The first conditional is used to make predictions and to talk about future actions or events which will probably happen. It is formed by: *If* + present simple + *will* + verb base form/infinitive without to.

If		present simple		subject		will	verb
If	you	place	a	plant cell	in water, it	will	become
If	there	is	enough light	stomata of a plant		will	open.

It is possible to start with the *will* clause.

> Stomata of a plant *will* open *if* there is enough light.
> A plant cell *will* become more turgid *if* it is placed in water.
> *If* there is enough light, stomata of a plant *will* open.

The second conditional

The second conditional tense is used to imagine situations in the present or the future that are very unlikely to happen or are impossible. It is formed by: *if* + past simple + *would* + verb base form/infinitive.

If		past simple		would	Infinitive verb	
If	there	were	no more eucalyptus plants in the world, koalas	would	become	extinct.
If	apple snails	disappeared	from this planet, snail kites	would	struggle	to survive.

It is possible to start with the *would* clause.

> Koalas *would* become extinct *if* there were no more eucalyptus plants in the world.
> Snail kites *would* struggle to survive *if* apple snails disappeared from this planet.

The passive voice

Passives are used when we want to talk about what action has happened rather than who did the action. Passives can be formed using any tense.

The present simple passive voice is used to talk about facts and is formed by *is/are* + past participle. If who or what caused the action is needed, you can use *is* + past participle + *by* + (who or what).

> Carbohydrates *are broken* down to glucose.
> Starch *is broken* down *by* amylase.
> Proteins *are broken* down *by* protease enzymes.
> Lipids *are broken* down *by* lipase enzymes.

The past passive voice is used to report what has happened and is formed by *was/were* + past participle.

> The fruit *was cut in half.*
> The acid *was added* to the fruit.
> The powder was *dissolved* in water.
> The results of the experiment *were recorded.*

We can change the passive voice back into the active voice.

Passive	Active
The fruit was cut in half.	I cut the fruit in half.
The acid was added to the fruit.	He added acid to the fruit.
The powder was dissolved in water.	They dissolved the powder in water.
The results of the experiment were recorded.	We recorded the results of the experiment.

In the active voice sentence, the subject of the sentence is performing the action. (Who did what.)

In the passive voice, the subject of the sentence has something done to it by someone or something. (What was done to whom or what.)

> The *diseased* cell. The *relaxed* muscle.

Modal verbs

Modal verbs are used to show possibility, likelihood, obligation, ability, permission, request, suggestions and to give advice. They do not change for *I, you, we, they, he, she, it*, and *they* do not use *do/does* in negatives and questions. Some examples of modal verbs are *could, should, would, might*.

Modal verbs are always followed by the base form of the verb.

> You *should see* the temperature rise.
> It *could take* a long time.

Modal verbs used to express how likely things are to happen or their probability are *could, should, likely to be* and *unlikely to*.

> Most fish are *unlikely to* survive being out of water for long.
> Life on Earth *could* not exist without the Sun.
> Genetics are more *likely to* be influential than the environment.
> Heart rate *should* decrease after exercise.

Will and *will not*

Will can be used in a statement to express certainty. *Will* comes after the subject and before another verb. If you want to make a negative statement, use *will not*. *Will not* can be shortened to *won't*.

> The molecules in cell B *will* diffuse down the concentration gradient to cell A.
> The molecules in cell A *will not* diffuse down the concentration gradient to cell B.

Giving advice

There are many different ways to give advice. *Should, ought to* and something *is good for you* are common ways to offer advice. You can use the negatives of these words and phrases to advise not to do something, for example *should not (shouldn't)* means something *is bad for you*. Note that *ought not* or *oughtn't* is rarely used in written English.

A gerund is a verb + *-ing*, which works like a noun in a sentence. An infinitive verb is the base form of the verb, for example *eat, run, drink*.

Should and *ought to* are followed by an infinitive verb.

A noun or verb + *-ing* comes before *is good for you* and *is bad for you*.

> You *should* eat lots of fresh fruit and vegetables to be healthy.
> You *ought to* drink plenty of water to be healthy.
> Exercise *is good for you.*
> Taking regular exercise *is good for you.*
> You *should not* eat too much processed food.
> Sugar is *bad for you.*
> Eating too much sugar is *bad for you.*

Some verbs are often followed by *to*, for example:

Verb	to	Example sentence
want		I *want to* eat more healthily.
try		I *try to* drink plenty of water.
need	to	I *need to* do more exercise.
have		I *have to get* healthier.
ought		I *ought to* eat less cake.

Words such as *should, would, could, might, can* and *will* are called modal verbs. Modal verbs are never followed by *to*. They are always followed by the base form of the verb.

You *should eat* a balanced diet.

I *will improve* my diet.

I *might drink* more fruit juice.

Nouns

Countable and uncountable nouns

Remember that a noun is the name of a person, animal, object, process or concept. There are countable nouns, for example, one *plant*, two *plants*, one *reptile*, two *reptiles*. Other nouns are uncountable and usually include liquids, powders, material, substances and concepts, for example *water*, *flour*, *rock*, *chocolate* and *advice*.

With countable nouns, use *a*, *an* or a number.

Countable nouns		Uncountable nouns	
	Used for		Used for
Some	positive statements	Some	positive statements
A few	positive statements	A little	positive statements
Plenty of	positive statements	Plenty of	positive statements
Lots of / a lot of	positive statements	Lots of / a lot of	positive statements
Any	negative statements and questions	Any	negative statements and questions
Many	negative statements and questions	Much	negative statements and questions

Countable nouns

There are *some* plants.

This plant has a *few* leaves.

There are *plenty* of leaves on this plant.

There are *a lot* of healthy plants.

There aren't *many* healthy plants.

Are there *any* healthy plants?

There aren't *many reptiles* in this area.

Are there *many* reptiles in this area?

Uncountable nouns

There is *some* water.

There is *a little* flour.

There is *plenty of* advice on the website.

There is *lots of* information on the website.

There isn't *any* rock in this area.

Is there *any* rock in this area?

There is not *much* chocolate left.

Is there *much* chocolate left?

To compare countable and uncountable nouns, use *more*, *less* and *fewer*. *More* is used with both countable and uncountable nouns. *Less* is used with uncountable nouns and *fewer* is used with countable nouns.

There are *more* leaves on this plant.

This plant has had *more* water than that plant.

This plant has had *less* sunlight than that plant.

There are *fewer* lizards on this island than before.

Plural nouns

Nouns in English are either singular, one, or plural, more than one. A common way to show a plural is to add -*s* or -*es* to the singular. For example, one cell, two cells. There are many irregular plurals, in other words, we create the plural form in another way. Many words in the English language are borrowed from other languages.

Many words in biology and other sciences come from Latin or Greek. These plurals are irregular.

	Singular	Plural
-us to *-i*	bronchus	bronchi
	alveolus	alveoli
-a to *-ae*	formula	formulae
	antenna	antennae
-um to *-a*	bacterium	bacteria

A *bronchus* is an airway in the breathing system that conducts air into the lungs.
There are two *bronchi*.

The *antennae* are organs located near the front of an insect's head. Each *antenna* can sense smell.

Bacteria are single-celled organisms with a simple internal structure with
no nucleus and they contain DNA.

Indefinite articles: *a* and *an*

The indefinite articles *a* and *an* are used to talk about one of something, which is general rather than specific. *A* is used before nouns that start with a consonant sound, and *an* is used before nouns that start with a vowel sound.

A large organ → An organ

A plant cell → An animal cell

Be careful because some words start with a vowel letter, but have a consonant sound, for example 'a one-celled organism'. Here the word 'one' starts with a *w* sound, so you must use *an* before it. Another example is 'unique'; this starts with a *y* sound, so you must say '*a* unique cell'.

Words that start with a consonant letter can sometimes have a vowel sound, for example 'hour'. This word starts with a silent *h* so you must say '*an* hour'.

The definite article: *the*

The definite article *the* is used to talk about singular, plural and uncountable nouns that are specific rather than general, or are known to the speaker or reader.

A skull is made of eight bones which protect our brain. *The* skull initially has soft spots which harden and fuse together within 18 months.

Please pass me the book. (The book we can both see.)

Pronouns: *this* and *these*

When it is clear what is being referred to, we can replace nouns, or the names of things, with pronouns. The pronoun *this* refers to a singular thing, and *these* is used to talk about plural objects. *This* and *these* can be used to talk about things that are physically near to us or are near in time.

An experiment is carried out to measure the effect of exercise on heart rate. *This* experiment is carried out using a running machine. (*This* indicates the experiment in the sentence before.)

There are many species of animals in this area. *This* means the environment has a high biodiversity. (*This* refers to the nearest fact to the word this, in this case the abundance of animals.)

This can be followed by verbs, as well as nouns.

	Noun		Verb
This	experiment	This	means
	system		occurs
	cell		carries

This experiment is useful. *This* means the results will help us to understand.

The breathing system is the network of organs and tissues that help you breathe. *This* system is vital for life.

There are many different cells in the body, one important cell is the red blood cell. *This* cell carries oxygen from the lungs.

Connectives

Connectives are words that join two parts of a sentence together, for example *and, or, so*. Some connectives show contrast or differences between two or more things, for example *but* and *however*. *While* and *whereas* also show the contrast between two things. *While* can be used for time and contrast. When it is used to show contrast, it has the same meaning as *whereas*. *While* and *whereas* can be used at the start of a sentence, or in the middle of a sentence after a comma.

But and *however* are used to link an affirmative and a negative together. *But* and *however* go before the negative part of the sentence.

Affirmative + *but* + negative.

Affirmative + *however* + negative.

Plant cells have chloroplasts, *but* animal cells do not.

Plant cells normally have one or more large vacuole(s), *however* animal cells have small vacuoles, if any at all.

Teeth do not contain bone marrow, *while* bones do.

Bones heal when broken, *whereas* teeth do not.

While bones grow and change with your body, teeth do not.

Whereas the bone marrow in bones produces red and white blood cells, teeth do not.

You can use *both* to talk about things which have similarities.

These two cells *both* have a cell wall.

Other connectives are used to give results or a conclusion, for example *therefore, consequently, so* and *which suggests*.

You can start a new sentence with *Therefore* or *Consequently*, for example.

> The leaves on this plant look healthy. *Consequently*, they must be getting enough water and nutrients.
> The plant has yellow leaves. *Therefore*, the plant must be deficient in light.

Which suggests and *so* are used to connect the two parts of the sentence.

> This plant looks healthy, *which suggests* it must be getting enough water and nutrients.
> This plant looks healthy, *so* it must be getting enough water and nutrients.

Because, *so* and *consequently* are used to show cause and effect. *Consequently* and *so* are used before the cause clause and *because* is used before the effect clause. In this type of sentence, there are two clauses or parts, the cause clause and the effect clause.

Because of, *due to* and *(be) caused by* can also be used to show cause and effect. These connectives can be followed by a noun phrase or verb + *-ing*.

Cause clause	Connective	Effect clause
Red blood cells are important for physical activity	*because*	they contain haemoglobin.
Arteries have a small lumen,	*so*	blood is pumped at high pressure.
Arteries have a small lumen.	*Consequently*,	blood is pumped at high pressure.
Blood is pumped at high pressure	*because of*	arteries having a small lumen.
Rapid diffusion of oxygen is possible	*due to*	red blood cells having a large surface area.
Blood vessels close to the surface of the skin enlarge	*(be) caused by*	heat.

Connective	Effect clause	Cause clause
Because	red blood cells contain haemoglobin,	they are important for physical activity.

Connectives to show sequence

Connectives have many uses. We can use the connectives, *first*, *then*, *next*, *after that* and *finally* to show a logical sequence of events or processes.

For example:

1   Pollen must be transferred from another plant.
2   The nucleus of the pollen grain travels down the pollen tube and fertilises the nucleus in the ovule.
3   The fertilised ovule develops into a seed. The seed contains the plant embryo. The ovary develops into the fruit.

> *First*, pollen must be transferred from another plant. *Next*, the pollen nucleus travels down the pollen tube and fertilises the nucleus in the ovule. *After that*, the fertilised ovule develops into a seed, which contains the plant embryo. *Finally*, the ovary develops into the fruit.

To show a result, we can use the connectives: *as a result*, *this means*, *finally* and *consequently*. The connectives usually go at the beginning of the sentence and make it clear to the reader in which order the events happened.

> Pollen is transferred to another plant. *As a result*, pollination takes place.

Connectives to give a reason

Connectives like *as*, *because*, *so that* and *in order that* are used to give a reason or to explain why something happens, and will usually follow a fact or an observation.

> Lungfish can survive droughts, *as* they bury into mud to slow down their metabolism and emerge when there is water once again.
>
> The thorny devil lizard survives living in the desert *because* it collects water in its back.
>
> Emperor penguins have solid bones, *so that* they can cope with the extreme water pressures when they dive deep down.
>
> Caribou have hollow hairs *in order that* they can survive extremely low temperatures.

Exemplification

In science, it is important to give examples of what you are talking about. You can use *for example*, *for instance*, *such as* and *including* to give examples.

> I noticed some changes, *for example*, as the temperature increased, the rate of reaction increased.
>
> Enzymes are used for many purposes, *such as* to remove stains from clothing, soften leather and ease digestion.
>
> Many companies use enzymes, *for instance*, pharmaceutical companies, laundry powder manufacturers and baby milk manufacturers.
>
> There are different types of enzymes, *including* lipase, protease and amylase.

Comparisons

When we compare two things, it is called an *analogy*. Useful phrases to show that two things have features that are alike, are *like*, *similar to* or *different to* and *different from*. *To* or *from* can be used after *different* as they have the same meaning.

Another way to talk about differences is by using *more than* and *less than* to compare things.

More … than and *less … than* are often used with adjectives to form comparative adjectives, but they are also used with nouns (sweat, energy) to imply a difference in quantity of something.

> Person A excretes *more* sweat than person B.
>
> This process requires *less* energy *than* other processes.

Also remember that after a statement or description, you can use *but* and an auxiliary verb to express contrast. The auxiliary (*does*, *did*, *has*, etc.) will be in the same tense as the verb in the first part of the sentence, but one will be positive, and one will be negative.

Groups of organisms which are more closely related have base sequences in DNA that are more *similar* to each other than those that share only a distant ancestor.
A plant cell is *different from* an animal cell.

Command words

When you are asked to *describe* something, write or say what you can see.

If you are asked to *explain* something, write or say how or why something has happened.

Describe

Substances move in and out of cells by diffusion.
Osmosis is the movement of water molecules.

Explain

Substances move in and out of cells by diffusion down a concentration gradient, through a partially permeable membrane.

Word order in sentences

There are different parts of a sentence, for example, the subject, the verb, and usually the object. The subject is usually a *noun* – a word that names a person, place or thing. The *verb* usually follows the subject and tells us an action or a state of being. An *object* receives the action and usually follows the verb.

Noun	Verb	
Diffusion	is	the movement of substances in and out of cells.
Active transport	requires	energy.
Osmosis	is	the movement of water across a partially permeable membrane.

Imperatives

Imperatives are used to give commands and orders. Imperative sentences start with a verb.

Cut the fruit in half.

Add the acid to the fruit.

Dissolve the powder in water.

Record the results of the experiment.

Synonyms

There are many words in English which mean the same thing, these words are called synonyms. Often, there are informal and formal synonyms. Usually, formal words are just one word, but the informal synonym is often a two-word phrase.

Formal	Informal
provide	give
perform	do, carry out
place	put, position
denature	stop functioning
increase	go up
decrease	go down
observe	look at
record	write down

Formal	Informal
The enzyme *denatured* at 38 °C.	The enzyme *stopped working* at 38 °C.
The results *provided* evidence of the temperatures *increasing*.	The results *gave* evidence of the temperatures *going up*.
I *recorded* the results accurately.	I *wrote down* the results carefully.

Affect and *effect*

Affect and *effect* look very similar, but *affect* is usually a verb in a sentence and *effect* is usually a noun.

Affect means to make a change in something. *Effect* means the result of the changes.

The *effect* of temperature on enzymes is that it will change its shape.

High temperatures will *affect* the shape of the enzyme.

Advice and *advise*

Advice is a noun and advise is a verb.

I can give you some *advice*.

I will *advise* you what to do.

Prefixes and suffixes

Prefixes

Prefixes are two or more letters which are added to the beginning of a word. They make a new word with a different meaning, for example, make the opposite meaning of the original word, make a word negative or express relations of time, place or manner.

Common prefixes used to describe numbers are *mono, di, tri* and *poly*.

Prefix	Meaning
Mono	1
Di	2
Tri	3
Poly	many

Monocot is a seed with one cotyledon.

Dicot is a seed with two cotyledons.

Trisomy is the condition of having three copies of a particular chromosome instead of two.

A *polypeptide* is a long, continuous chain of amino acids, for example protein is a polypeptide.

Prefix	Meaning	Examples
Homo-	the same	A bat's wing and a human's arm are homologous structures.
Geno-	related to family or birth	Your genotype is inherited from your parents.
Pheno-	to show	Phenotypes are the characteristics that you can see of living things, for example the colour of the hair and eyes.
Centro-	related to the centre of something	The centromere is the central joining point of chromatids.

You do not need to know any details of the terms homologous, centromere and chromatid, as they are beyond the requirements of the syllabus.

Some prefixes are used to create a negative meaning, for example *in-* and *im-*. The prefix *in-* changes to *im-* before words that begin with the letters *p* and *m*.

in-	
affirmative	negative
organic	inorganic
dependent	independent
active	inactive

im-	
affirmative	negative
perfect	imperfect
possible	impossible
mature	immature

Living creatures are made of different types of organic compounds.
*In*organic molecules are made of elements, such as hydrogen or carbon.

Suffixes: adding *-s* or *-es*

A letter or letters added to the end of root words are called *suffixes*.

Adding the suffix *-s* or *-es* to the end of English words has many different purposes and it is important to know how to use them.

You have seen that these suffixes are used when we use verbs together with *he*, *she* and *it*, for example, *it boils* or *he watches*. This is called the third person *s*.

We can also add *-s* or *-es* to the end of nouns to make plurals:

Singular	Plural	Spelling rule
Thermometer	Thermometers	Just add 's'
Kidney	kidneys	Vowel + y = just add 's'
Baby	Babies	Consonant + y = change the 'y' to an 'i' and add 'es'
Tube	Tubes	End in 'e' = just add 's'
cervix	cervixes	End in s, ch, sh, x, z = +es
calf	calves	End in 'f' = change the 'f' to a 'v' and add 'es'

Possessive *-s*

Another use of *-s* is to show possession.

The liver*'s* role. (The role of the liver.)
We have two kidney*s*. (Singular, regular noun.)
The kidney*s'* blood supply comes via the renal arteries. (Plural, regular noun.)
The children*'s* growth rate is measured. (Irregular plural noun: one child, two children.)

It's and *its* works a bit differently. *It's* is short for *it is* or *it has*, while *its* is used to express possession.

The liver is an important organ. *Its* function is to regulate chemical levels in the blood and excrete a bile.
A giraffe has a long neck. *It's* (it has) adapted to eat leaves from the top of tall trees.

Changing verbs into nouns

Some verbs can be changed into nouns by adding -*ion*.

Verb	Noun
act	action
react	reaction
digest	digestion
ingest	ingestion
absorb	absorption

Mostly, -*ion* can be added to the verb, but notice that the letter *b* in absorb changes to a *p* in the noun *absorption*.

> My body *reacts* to certain food. → I have an allergic *reaction* when I eat nuts.
>
> I must *act* quickly if my allergy starts. → The best *action* is to avoid eating nuts.
>
> I cannot *digest* meat very well. → My *digestion* system is sensitive.
>
> I don't like to *ingest* citrus fruits. → *Ingestion* is when food, drink or another substance is taken into the body by swallowing or absorbing it.

Word families and suffixes

The end of a word can inform you what type of word it is. A root word means the shortest version of a word. Letters can be added to the end of many root words to change the type of word it is. If you add -*ion*, -*tion* or -*sion* to the end of a root word, it creates a noun. For example, *infect* (verb), *infection* (noun).

Adding -*ed* to a root word can show the past tense of a verb, but it can also create an adjective, for example, *infected* wound.

Prepositions

Prepositions are small words that are used with nouns and pronouns to show place, direction and the relationship to another word.

Preposition	Meaning
Away (from)	To leave the starting point
into	Within or inside
out	Stop being inside something or somewhere and leave.
to	Travel in the direction of or to a destination or place (the end destination is important)
towards	Travel in the direction of (the journey is important)

Arteries carry oxygen *away from* the heart.

We breathe air containing oxygen *into* our lungs.

We breathe *out* air containing carbon dioxide.

Our lungs supply oxygen *to* the cells via the blood and cardiovascular system.

Blood flows *towards* the heart and enters through two large veins.

Adverbs of manner

Adverbs of manner are used to give more information about a verb, and they say how an action is done. Most adverbs are formed by adding *-ly to adjectives.*

The heart beats *quickly* during exercise.

If the temperature *suddenly* rises, our skin reacts by producing sweat.

Children get *increasingly* taller as they get older.

You can *easily* recognise insects by the antennae, six legs and wings.

You must record the results of the experiment *carefully*.

You must think *scientifically*.

For adjectives that end with *-y*, change the *y* to *i*, so *busy → busily.*

For adjectives that end with *-l*, double the *-l*, so *general → generally.*

For adjectives that end with *-ic*, add *ally*, so *specific → specifically.*

There are some irregular adverbs that do not end in *-ly.* These include *fast, hard, well.*

He did the experiment *well.*

Describing graphs

There are specific words to label different parts of a graph. The table below gives some terms that are used to label graphs, and their meanings.

Term	Meaning
axis/axes (x-axis, y-axis)	The vertical line (from top to bottom) on a graph is usually called the y-axis and the x-axis is usually the line from side-to-side.
gradient	A gradient is the line drawn on the graph. The higher the gradient of a graph, the steeper the line is. If a line slopes downwards, it shows a negative gradient.
curve	A curved line on a graph means that the gradient, or rate of change, is always changing.
line	A line connects points on a graph.
points	The points on a graph are the coordinates, or the place on the graph where dots are drawn to plot the results.
origin	The origin on a graph is the starting point, in other words, 0 on the x-axis and 0 on the y-axis.
intersect	To intersect is when there are two or more lines on a graph, and they cross each other. They intersect at this point.

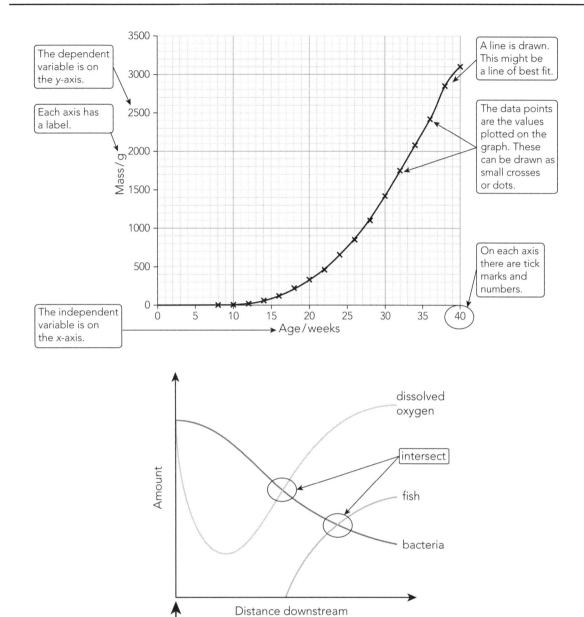

The dependent variable is on the y-axis.

Each axis has a label.

The independent variable is on the x-axis.

A line is drawn. This might be a line of best fit.

The data points are the values plotted on the graph. These can be drawn as small crosses or dots.

On each axis there are tick marks and numbers.

Mass / g

Age / weeks

dissolved oxygen

intersect

fish

bacteria

Amount

Distance downstream

point at which untreated sewage is discharged

Characteristics and classification of living organisms

IN THIS CHAPTER YOU WILL:

Science skills:

- use a dichotomous key

- identify the characteristics of living organisms.

English skills:

- use the present tense and descriptive words to talk about living organisms.

Exercise 1.1 Characteristics of living organisms

IN THIS EXERCISE YOU WILL:

Science skills:

- identify the seven characteristics of living organisms.

English skills:

- list the key words associated with living organisms.

KEY WORD

characteristics: visible features of an organism

All living organisms share the same seven **characteristics** of life. We do not consider them to be 'alive' if they do not have all seven. This exercise will help you to identify the seven characteristics of life.

1 Look for and circle the names of the seven characteristics for living things in this word search puzzle. You will also find the scientific term for a living thing in the word search.

P	M	K	X	A	F	H	R	A	Z	E	O	P	V	W
N	S	O	O	T	T	Z	H	F	X	X	R	S	D	Z
X	V	O	V	W	M	L	L	P	F	F	G	D	U	D
U	Q	Y	O	E	Y	X	R	B	P	I	A	S	X	N
D	R	R	Y	N	M	O	Q	A	I	T	N	E	H	U
C	G	E	B	N	J	E	I	S	W	J	I	N	G	T
H	W	W	S	E	E	Z	N	H	J	P	S	S	K	R
K	S	J	E	P	O	S	Q	T	O	R	M	I	U	I
O	G	N	U	X	I	E	R	D	X	A	O	T	K	T
D	K	J	O	Q	N	R	P	K	P	D	N	I	S	I
D	O	X	Q	B	C	T	A	D	V	J	F	V	Z	O
R	E	P	R	O	D	U	C	T	I	O	N	I	Z	N
M	B	J	W	Q	I	P	B	P	I	F	Q	T	B	N
T	K	V	I	L	O	E	Z	M	H	O	L	Y	B	T
H	H	G	E	X	C	R	E	T	I	O	N	A	R	G

2 Use the eight words from the word search puzzle to complete the table.
Match the words to the definition of each word.

Definition	Word
a living thing	
an action by an organism or part of an organism causing a change of position or place	
the chemical reactions in cells that break down nutrient molecules and release energy for metabolism	
the ability to detect and respond to changes in the internal or external environment	
a permanent increase in size and dry mass	
the processes that make more of the same kind of organism	
the removal of the waste products of metabolism and substances in excess of requirements	
taking in materials for energy, growth and development	

Exercise 1.2 Constructing a key – writing opposites

IN THIS EXERCISE YOU WILL:

Science skills:

- complete a dichotomous key.

English skills:

- use opposites in sentences.

KEY WORDS

dichotomous key: a way of identifying an organism, by working through pairs of statements that lead you to its name

Making comparisons is an important skills that is essential when constructing a **dichotomous key**.

If you don't know the name of an organism, or what group it belongs to, you can use a dichotomous key which consists of pairs of definitions. When you choose the definition that matches your organism, you are led to the next choice. In the end, you get the name of your organism or the group it belongs to.

The person using the key should be able to identify the species or organism that they are observing. Each part of the key should be written using opposites to decide if a particular characteristic is present or not. For example:

The organism *has* jointed limbs.

The organism *does not have* jointed limbs.

This allows the user of the key to observe whether the organism has jointed limbs or not before moving onto the next statement.

3   Complete the sentences below with suitable opposites. The first example has been done for you.

   i   The organism has fur.

   The organism does not have fur.

   ii   The organism has feathers.

   ....

   iii   ....

   The organism does not fertilise externally.

   iv   The adult organism has gills.

   ....

Exercise 1.3 Describing organisms

IN THIS EXERCISE YOU WILL:

Science skills:

- identify key characteristics of birds.

English skills:

- extract important information from a text or a diagram.

KEY WORD

vertebrate: an organism that has a backbone/spinal cord, such as mammals, amphibians, birds, reptiles and fish

Birds are one of the main vertebrate groups in the animal kingdom. Read the text and look at Figure 1.1 to learn some characteristics of birds. Then extract key information from the text and the diagram to answer the questions that follow. Finding information in a text or article is an important skill in biology.

Birds such as the finch (*Fringillidae*) are **vertebrates** and belong to the class *Aves* (birds) in the phylum *Chordata* of the animal kingdom. Birds have lungs, feathers and beaks as common observable characteristics. Like humans, birds are required to maintain their internal body temperature and are considered to be homeotherms. Birds are similar to reptiles in that they can reproduce by internal fertilisation and lay eggs.

You do not need to know any details of the terms homeotherm, class and phylum, as they are beyond the requirements of the syllabus.

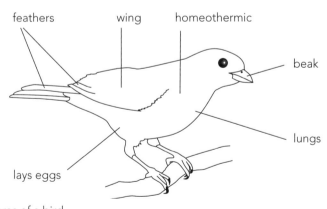

Figure 1.1: Features of a bird.

4 Identify the class that birds belong to. ....

5 List three observable characteristics that birds have.

....

....

....

6 State the word that describes birds being able to maintain their body temperature.

....

7 Identify the type of fertilisation that birds use to reproduce. ....

LANGUAGE TIP

Some verbs like *State*, *Identify*, and *List* are useful to understand because they tell you what you need to do to answer a question. Find examples of other verbs in the exercises so far and write down what the verb means. This will help you to understand them as you see them throughout the book.

LANGUAGE FOCUS

The present simple is the tense we use to state facts that are always true:

'Birds have feathers.' and 'Fish live in water.' = facts about birds and fish – they are characteristics.

For affirmative sentences, use subject + infinitive (+ object)(+ adverb).

If the subject is the 3rd person singular – a bird, a fish – add -s or -es. So, *A fish lives in water.*

Verbs that end with -s, -z, -tch, -ch or -sh need -es. So, *An eagle catches a fish.*

Have is an irregular verb; the 3rd person form is *has*. So, *A bird has feathers.*

For negative sentences, use subject + don't / doesn't (+ object)(+ adverb):

Birds don't live in water. A fish doesn't have feathers.

Exercise 1.4 Kingdom to species

IN THIS EXERCISE YOU WILL:

Science skills:

- list the order of classification for an organism.

English skills:

- write sentences to explain how different organisms are grouped together.

When reading about different organisms and species, you need to remember the order of classification from kingdom to species:

- kingdom
- phylum
- class
- order
- family
- genus
- species.

> You do not need to know any details of the terms phylum, class, order and family, as they are beyond the requirements of the syllabus.

Using these terms in your own writing is more difficult. This exercise will help you to use the different levels of organisation in your writing.

8   Complete the description of the organism using the words below.
The text follows the order of classification from kingdom to species.

binomial   characteristic   classification

genus   kingdom   species

Allium sativum is more commonly known as garlic and is a member of the

plantae .... The seeds of garlic are displayed externally and this

.... places garlic into the *spermatophyta* phylum. Garlic belongs to

the *liliopsida* class and the *asparagales* order. The next level in the ....

of garlic is the *Alliaceae* family. The .... name of garlic is *Allium*

sativum, which means that the .... name is *Allium* and the

.... is *sativum*.

9   Now it is your turn to construct a description of an organism. You can use the text about garlic in question **8** to help you. Choose an organism that interests you and research the information you need in books or on the internet.

Include the following information in your description:

- At least three observable characteristics of your chosen organism that explain why it belongs to a particular group. Examples may include the kingdom, the genus, the species.

Use the space below to complete your answer:

....

....

....

....

....

....

....

....

....

....

....

› Chapter 2
Cells

Exercise 2.1 The parts of a cell

You should be able to describe the general function of the different parts of a cell in this exercise.

1   Some parts of cells are labelled in Figure 2.1. Write the name of each part next to the correct definition below.

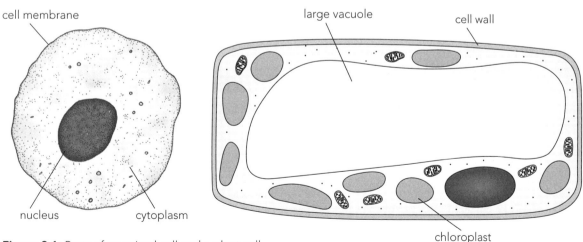

Figure 2.1: Parts of an animal cell and a plant cell.

a   A fluid-filled space inside a cell, separated from the cytoplasm

by a membrane. ....

b   Substances can pass in and out of the cell through this. ....

c   Made of cellulose and gives strength to the cell. ....

d   A substance like jelly that fills the cell. ....

e   Stores genetic information. ....

f   Absorbs sunlight for photosynthesis. ....

2   Some of the structures in question **1** are only found in plant cells, and some
are found in plant *and* animal cells. Write the names of the seven structures in
question **1** in the correct column below. Two have been done for you.

Plant cell only	Plant cell and animal cell
large vacuole	cell membrane

Exercise 2.2 Comparing cells

IN THIS EXERCISE YOU WILL:

Science skills:

- compare the structure of different cells.

English skills:

- describe differences using sentences expressing contrast.

KEY WORDS

cell wall: a tough layer outside the cell membrane; found in the cells of
plants, fungi and bacteria

nucleus: a structure containing DNA in the form of chromosomes

You will often need to compare the structure of different cells. This exercise will give
you practice in using the correct language for making comparisons.

LANGUAGE FOCUS

To describe differences and contrast two things, you can use phrases like:

Cell A has a vacuole, **but** *cell B does not.*

Cell A has a vacuole, **however** *cell B does not.*

The above sentences describe differences between two cells.

To express and emphasise similarity, you can use *both*:

The two cells both contain a cell membrane.

3   Look at Figures 2.2–2.7. Complete the sentences to describe similarities or differences between the cells.

Here is an example to help you.

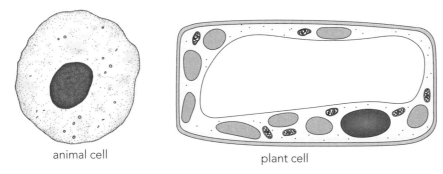

animal cell   plant cell

Figure 2.2: An animal cell and a plant cell.

The plant cell has a **cell wall**, but the animal cell does not.

a

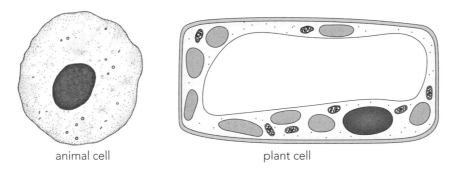

animal cell   plant cell

Figure 2.3: An animal cell and a plant cell.

The plant cell and the animal cell .... a **nucleus**.

b

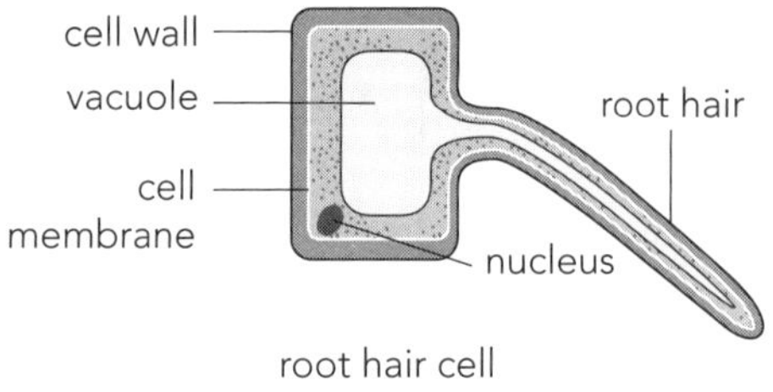

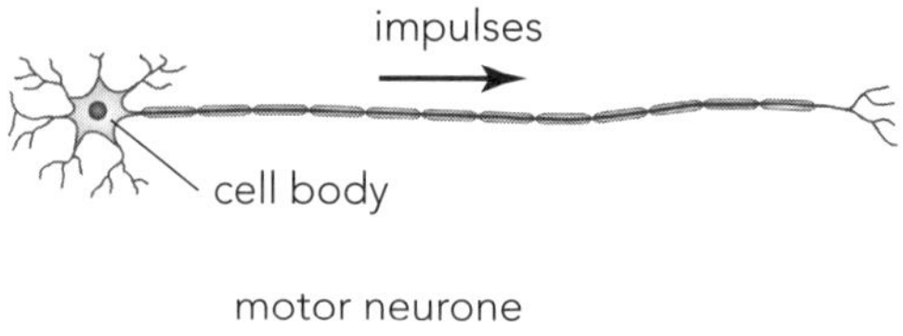

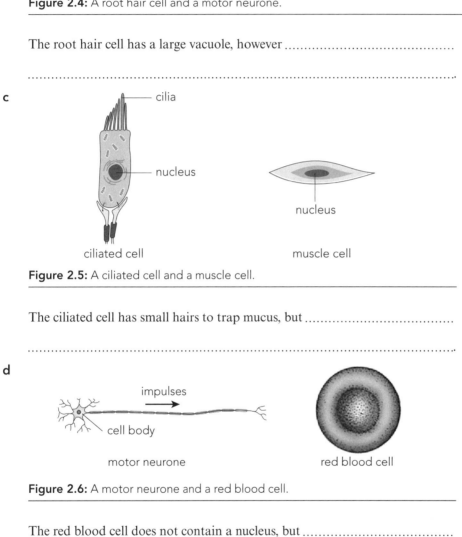

Figure 2.4: A root hair cell and a motor neurone.

The root hair cell has a large vacuole, however ....

....

c

Figure 2.5: A ciliated cell and a muscle cell.

The ciliated cell has small hairs to trap mucus, but ....

....

d

Figure 2.6: A motor neurone and a red blood cell.

The red blood cell does not contain a nucleus, but ....

....

e   Now write a complete sentence of your own comparing animal and plant cells.

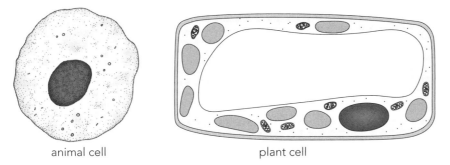

animal cell   plant cell

Figure 2.7: An animal cell and a plant cell.

....

....

Exercise 2.3 Organisation of cells

IN THIS EXERCISE YOU WILL:

Science skills:

• describe the hierarchy of cell organisation.

English skills:

• use 'an' and 'a' before the appropriate word.

KEY WORDS

organ: a group of tissues that work together to perform a particular function

organ system: several organs that work together to perform a particular function

specialised cell: a cell that is responsible for a particular function. An example of a specialised cell is a red blood cell. The function of a red blood cell is to carry oxygen around the body

tissue: a group of similar cells that work together to perform a particular function

This exercise will help you to describe specific cells, tissues, organs or organ systems with real examples from different organisms.

There are many different types of **specialised cell** in an organism. Cells that have a similar structure and function work together as a **tissue**. Several tissues may combine to form **organs**. Organs work together in **organ systems**. A collection of organ systems forms an organism.

cells	▶	tissues	▶	organs	▶	organ systems

4 Choose the correct term to complete the following sentences. Cross out the incorrect term(s). Here is an example to help you:

A leaf is an example of **a tissue** / ~~an organ~~ found in many types of plant.

a The eye is a type of **cell** / **tissue** / **organ** found in many animals.

b A thin layer of **cells** / **tissues** called the epithelium gives protection to various parts of the body.

c The oesophagus, stomach, liver and pancreas are all **cells** / **tissues** / **organs** and are part of a typical digestive **system** / **body**.

d A root hair **cell** / **tissue** absorbs water and mineral ions for plants to use.

e The trachea contains ciliated **cells** / **tissues** that trap and remove mucus from the body.

f Blood is **a tissue** / **an organ** that contains red blood **cells** / **tissues**. It transports substances around the body.

g Muscle cells work together in muscle **tissue** / **organs** to allow the heart to pump blood around the body.

h The small intestine is a collection of tissues that work together as an **organ system** / **organ**. It digests food substances.

LANGUAGE FOCUS

Remember to use 'an' when the next word begins with a vowel *sound* (a, e, i, o or u). Use 'a' when the next word begins with a consonant *sound*. For example:

An organ   *An* unusual reaction   *An* hour-long experiment (silent h)

A cell   *A* unit (sounds like <u>y</u>unit)

Also, when words begin with single letters, think about the sound:

X-ray (eks-ray) = *an* X-ray

---

5 For the clues below, write your answer using 'a' or 'an' before the word. For example:

Contains the genetic information for the cell. .... *a nucleus* ....

a A thin layer that allows substances to pass through. ....

b Protects a cell. ....

c Stores genetic information. ....

d Absorbs sunlight for photosynthesis. ....

e Is made up from different cells and tissues. ....

LANGUAGE TIP

Some English words may look or sound like a word in another language you know and have the *same* meaning. Other English words may look or sound like words in another language but have a *different* meaning. Try to learn the ones with a different meaning: they are 'false friends'! Are there any 'false friends' in Exercise 2.3?

Movement into and out of cells

Science skills:

- describe how substances move into and out of cells.

English skills:

- write short sentences and paragraphs about diffusion

- know the difference between the command words 'describe' and 'explain' and use this to answer questions on osmosis.

Exercise 3.1 Key words

IN THIS EXERCISE YOU WILL:

Science skills:

- become familiar with the key words associated with movement into and out of cells.

English skills:

- reorder words in the correct order to form sentences.

KEY WORDS

active transport: the movement of molecules or ions through a cell membrane from a region of lower concentration to a region of higher concentration (i.e. against a concentration gradient) using energy from respiration

diffusion: the net movement of particles from a region of their higher concentration to a region of their lower concentration (i.e. down a concentration gradient), as a result of their random movement

osmosis: the diffusion of water molecules through a partially permeable membrane

This exercise will encourage you to use the important key words associated with the chapter. Many of the words might be new to you, but are appropriate for describing what happens to cells when substances move into and out of cells.

1   Reorder the letters to spell out the key words. Each word is associated with how substances can move into or out of cells.

   a   usidiffon   ....

   b   isossmo   ....

   c   twaer iapotlent   ....

   d   tacvei tnsprarto   ....

2   Reorder the words to form correct sentences about movement into and out of cells. Remember to add capital letters and full stops to your completed sentences.

   a   **diffusion** movement random involves of particles the

   b   **osmosis** the partially molecules is membrane water permeable a through of movement

   c   energy requires **active transport**

LANGUAGE TIP

Key words require regular practice. Make your own sentences and say them out loud to a classmate, and if they understand you then you have successfully mastered the key word.

Exercise 3.2 Describing diffusion

IN THIS EXERCISE YOU WILL:

Science skills:

- describe what happens to particles during diffusion.

English skills:

- use 'will' or 'will not' + verb for certainty.

KEY WORDS

concentration gradient: when the concentration of particles is different in one area than another

When you are learning about diffusion, it is important to be able to use your knowledge to describe what happens to the particles. It is also important to use the correct scientific language.

Diffusion is the movement of molecules from an area of high concentration to an area of low concentration (or down the **concentration gradient**). Diffusion is one way in which particles can move in and out of cells across the partially permeable cell membrane.

The diagrams in the questions show different situations where diffusion may take place. You will complete and write sentences that describe what will happen to the particles labelled. The following key words are available for you to use.

concentration gradient   **diffuse**   **high concentration**

low concentration   **(oxygen) molecules**   **partially permeable membrane**

Here is an example to help you:

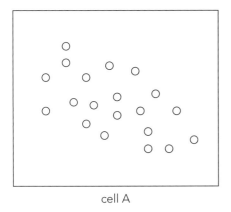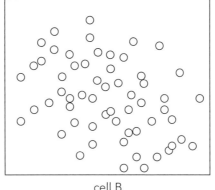

cell A   cell B

Figure 3.1: Diffusion in cells A and B.

Model sentences:

The **molecules** in cell B will **diffuse** down the **concentration gradient** to cell A.

Or:

The **molecules** will move from a **high concentration** in cell B to a **lower concentration** in cell A.

3   Look at Figure 3.2, then complete the sentences below by circling the correct option.

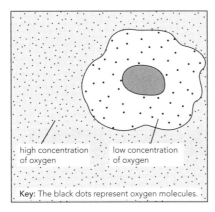

high concentration of oxygen   low concentration of oxygen

Key: The black dots represent oxygen molecules.

Figure 3.2: Diffusion diagram.

LANGUAGE TIP

When you are certain about how something will act or react, use *will* or *will not* in front of the verb:

The molecules will move.

Diffusion will take place because the membrane is partially permeable.

Can you find two more examples in the paragraph in question **3**?

The concentration of oxygen molecules is **higher / lower** outside the cell than inside. This will cause the molecules of oxygen to move **into / out of** the cell. The oxygen molecules will **diffuse / transport** across the membrane. The membrane of the cell is **partially / fully** permeable so it will allow diffusion to take place.

4 Look at Figure 3.3. Write a short paragraph to describe what will happen to the oxygen molecules this time. Use the key words and the model sentences given to help you.

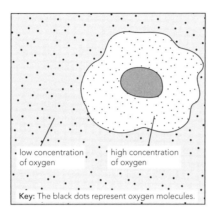

low concentration of oxygen

high concentration of oxygen

Key: The black dots represent oxygen molecules.

Figure 3.3: Diffusion diagram.

concentration   diffuse   lower   membrane   move out

outside   oxygen molecules   permeable

....

....

....

....

Exercise 3.3 Describing and explaining osmosis

IN THIS EXERCISE YOU WILL:

Science skills:

- explain what happens to water molecules during osmosis

- describe what happens during osmosis using data from a graph.

English skills:

- use the command term to understand what is required when answering a question.

This exercise focuses on the difference between the terms *describe* and *explain*. You will also improve your understanding of osmosis experiments, and your ability to use a graph.

'Describe' and 'explain' are common examples of command words.

Command terms are verbs used to give instructions, orders, or commands.

If you have to describe a graph, you should just write about what you see. Do not write about how or why the data shows what has happened. For example:

The concentration of water inside the cell increased after 30 seconds.

If you have to explain what you see in a graph, give the scientific reasons *how* or *why* something has happened. For example:

The concentration of water increased because water moved from an area of higher water concentration.

So, *describe* = what is it like, and *explain* = why, how.

for frequent 'science' verbs such as *provide* (= give), *perform* (= do or carry out) and *place* (= put), and make a list of them. For example:

Rain provides the trees with water. (= Rain gives the trees water.)

He placed the sample in the dish. (= He put the sample in the dish.)

The following paragraph *describes* and *explains* osmosis. Read the paragraph, then answer the questions below.

> Osmosis is the movement of water molecules through a partially permeable membrane down a concentration gradient. Cell membranes are partially permeable, so osmosis can occur through them. If a cell is placed in a solution that is more concentrated than the cytoplasm, water will move out of the cell. If a cell is placed in a solution that is less concentrated than the cytoplasm, water will move into the cell.

Zara performed an experiment to study osmosis. She placed a piece of potato in a concentrated sugar solution. She measured the mass of the potato every minute.

Figure 3.4 shows what Zara observed.

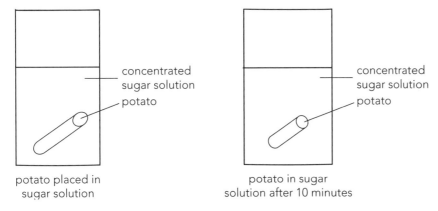

potato placed in
sugar solution

potato in sugar
solution after 10 minutes

Figure 3.4: Osmosis observations diagram.

Her results are shown in Table 3.1.

Time / minutes	Mass / g
0	3.6
2	3.6
4	3.5
6	3.1
8	2.7
10	2.5

Table 3.1: Mass of a potato placed into a solution.

Zara drew the graph in Figure 3.5 to present her results:

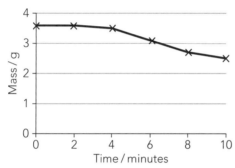

Figure 3.5: Graph of results.

5   Look at Zara's graph and describe what happens to the mass of the potato.
    At what time does the mass of the potato start changing?

    In general, the graph shows the change in ....

    ....

    Specifically, it can be observed that after .... minutes, ...

    ....

    ....

6   Explain what Zara's graph shows. Why has the mass of the potato changed?
    Use your knowledge of osmosis to explain this change.

    The mass of the potato has changed because ....

    ....

    ....

    ....

Chapter 4

Biological molecules

IN THIS CHAPTER YOU WILL:

Science skills:

- identify biological molecules and the key words associated with them
- construct a method for carrying out food tests.

English skills:

- use prefixes to deduce information about biological molecules
- use the imperative form when writing instructions and the passive form when describing what you did in an experiment.

Exercise 4.1 Chemicals of life – vocabulary

IN THIS EXERCISE YOU WILL:

Science skills:

- identify key words associated with biological molecules.

English skills:

- construct simple sentences about biological molecules.

It is useful for you to understand the key terms in this exercise and how they contribute to a healthy organism. Some of the terms are also used in chemistry.

1   Separate the words to make definitions. Then match the definitions with these words:

atom   carbohydrate   enzyme   metabolism

molecule   water

Here is an example to help you:

A / substance / that / cannot / be / broken / down / into /

anything / simpler.   *element*

a   Aproteinthatactsasabiologicalcatalyst.   ....

b   Asingleparticleofanelement.   ....

c   Twoormoreatomsjoinedtogether.   ....

d   Chemicalreactionsthattakeplaceinthebody.   ....

e   Ausefulsubstancethatmakesup80%ofthebody.   ....

f   Amoleculethatcontainscarbonhydrogenandoxygen.   ....

Exercise 4.2 Sentences about carbohydrates

IN THIS EXERCISE YOU WILL:

Science skills:

- identify types of carbohydrates.

English skills:

- use prefixes when naming carbohydrates.

KEY WORDS

carbohydrates: substances that include sugars, starch and cellulose; they contain carbon, hydrogen and oxygen

glucose: a sugar that is used in respiration to release energy

respiration: the chemical reactions in cells that break down nutrient molecules and release energy for metabolism

The different types of **carbohydrates** can be classified into groups depending on their structure. The clue to this is in their name. Carbohydrates are a class of substances that includes starches, sugars and cellulose.

LANGUAGE FOCUS

A prefix is a group of letters at the beginning of some words which tells you something about the meaning of the word. Many scientific words have prefixes, and some of those prefixes refer to numbers. For example:

mono- = one   *di-* = two   *tri-* = three   *poly-* = multiple

Monocotyledon refers to seeds that have one cotyledon only.

The tricuspid valve in the heart has three points.

The different sugars in the carbohydrate group can be described as *simple* or *complex* sugars. A simple or complex sugar will have a name that helps you to see this.

2   a   Complete the table below using the words given.

di-   glucose   maltose   many   monosaccharide

poly-   polysaccharide   starch   two

Prefix/meaning	Type of sugar	Example
mono-/one	....	....
.... /	disaccharide	sucrose and ....
.... /	....	cellulose and ....

b   Use two of the words again to complete the definition.

.... such as cellulose are made up of .... units of sugar

and resemble a long chain. This is why they are known as complex sugars.

3   **Glucose** is a carbohydrate that is vital to the chemical process of **respiration**. Respiration is the process in cells that breaks down nutrient molecules and releases energy for metabolism.

Complete these sentences about glucose by crossing out the incorrect terms.

Glucose is a **simple / complex** sugar that is made up of six **oxygen / carbon** atoms joined together in a ring. **Six / Twelve** hydrogen atoms are attached to the carbon atoms, as well as six **oxygen / hydrogen** atoms.

4   In Exercise 4.3, you are going to read about an experiment. Before you read, unscramble the words to make a definition of glucose. The first one has been done for you.

Glucose ($C_6H_{12}O_6$) is a **plisme edirahccaonosm** found in **lanspt**. It is absorbed directly into our **doolb** during digestion and is a vital source of **reneyg**.

Glucose ($C_6H_{12}O_6$) is a .....*simple*..... .... found in ....

It is absorbed directly into our .... during digestion and is a vital

source of ....

> You do not need to know any details of the terms monosaccharide and polysaccharide, as they are beyond the requirements of the syllabus.

LANGUAGE TIP

When you see 'as well as', it does not always have a meaning related to 'good', 'well' or 'efficiently'. It often means 'and' or 'also'.

Exercise 4.3 Planning a food test

IN THIS EXERCISE YOU WILL:

Science skills:

- construct a method for carrying out food tests.

English skills:

- write in instructions and a report
- complete sentences using the correct imperative
- rewrite instructions using the passive form.

KEY WORDS

Benedict's solution: a blue liquid that turns orange–red when heated with reducing sugar

5 a   Arun has written some instructions about how to test for the presence of glucose in a sample of food. However, the instructions are in the *wrong* order. Put the instructions in the correct order, numbering them from 1 to 8. The first has been done for you.

   A   Cut the food up into very small pieces.   ....

   B   Add **Benedict's solution** to the test-tube   ....

   C   Dissolve the food in water in a test-tube.   ....

   D   Record the results in the results table.   ....

   E   Collect the necessary equipment, including your safety spectacles.   ....1.....

   F   Draw a results table.   ....

   G   Observe whether the solution turns orange–red, showing glucose is present.   ....

   H   Strongly heat the test-tube in a water-bath.   ....

   b   Complete the sentences with the correct imperative:

add   collect   cut   dissolve

draw   heat   observe   record

   Food is .... into small pieces.

   You can .... a solution to a test-tube.

   A student will .... their results into a table.

   When an experiment begins, students will .... the correct equipment.

   When you add sugar to a hot drink, the sugar will ....

LANGUAGE FOCUS

When you write about an experiment in a report, an appropriate form is the past passive. Scientists often use the passive voice of the past, because the action is more important than the person (or 'agent') who performed it.

There are three simple steps to report experiment instructions in the passive form.

Here is an instruction: *Record the volume of water.*

To make this instruction passive:

1   Find the object of the sentence. The object is the 'thing' the verb acts on and is after the verb: the volume of water. This becomes the subject of the new sentence:

   The volume of water…

2   If the new subject is singular, add *was/was not*. If it is plural, add *were/ were not*:

   The volume of water was…

3   Finally, add the past participle of the verb. For regular verbs, add *-ed*. For irregular verbs, use the third form (think/thought/thought; see/saw/seen):

   The volume of water was recorded.

6   Rewrite Arun's instructions in the correct order and in the passive form. The first one has been done for you.

   a   The necessary equipment was collected, including our safety spectacles.

   b   The food ....

   c   ....

   d   ....

   e   ....

   f   ....

   g   ....

   h   ....

7 The series of diagrams shows you how to carry out simple food tests. Use the diagrams to answer the questions that follow.

a

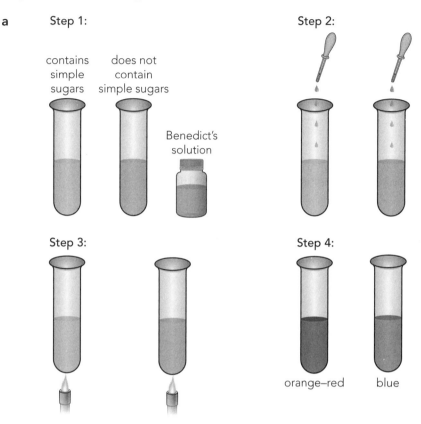

Figure 4.1: How to carry out a simple food test.

Complete the following sentences about the four stages of the food test.

i Step 1 shows a test-tube containing a solution of simple sugars.

.... is an example of a simple sugar.

ii Step 2 shows .... being added to the ....

iii Step 3 shows the test-tubes ....

iv Step 4 shows ....

....

....

....

v The solution in the test-tube that contains simple sugars has turned from

.... to ....

b

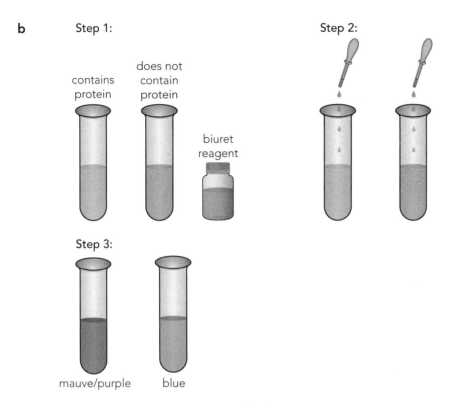

Figure 4.2: How to carry out a simple food test.

This time, you should write a full sentence of your own to describe what is happening at each step of the food test.

i Step 1 shows ....

....

....

ii Step 2 shows ....

....

iii Step 3 shows ....

....

iv Food test **b** shows that the presence of .... will turn

.... reagent from .... to ....

Chapter 5

Enzymes

IN THIS CHAPTER YOU WILL:

Science skills:

- develop your understanding of enzymes

- learn about how different enzymes are used in industry.

English skills:

- interpret a graph and use it to write sentences using correct scientific words or phrases

- understand the difference between 'affect' and 'effect'.

Exercise 5.1 Key words for enzymes

IN THIS EXERCISE YOU WILL:

Science skills:

- develop your understanding of how enzymes work.

English skills:

- use the correct word to complete sentences about enzymes.

KEY WORDS

enzymes: proteins that are involved in all metabolic reactions, where they function as biological catalysts

substrate: the substance that an enzyme causes to react

The study of **enzymes** is filled with specialised words. Understanding these important words will help you to answer questions related to enzymes and how they function. Enzymes make reactions happen faster when they combine with a **substrate** to produce products. These reactions happen more often at the correct temperature and pH levels.

If the temperature or pH is too low or too high, the enzyme will not work at its maximum rate.

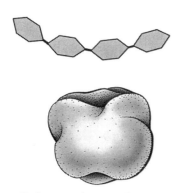  

Each enzyme has an active site into which its substrate molecule fits exactly. The enzyme here is amylase, and its active site is just the right size and shape for a starch molecule.

The substrate molecule (starch in this case) slots into the active site.

The starch is split into glucose molecules. The enzyme is unaltered, and ready to accept another part of the starch molecule.

Figure 5.1: How an enzyme works.

1   Find out the meanings of the words and use them to complete the passage with the correct key words about enzymes. There are two words that you do not need.

denatured   decreased   speed up   complementary   product

pH   temperature   optimum   catalysts   substrate

Enzymes are proteins which are biological .... This means that enzymes

can .... a chemical reaction. An enzyme will only work with a particular

.... – they are .... to each other. Once the reaction has taken

place at the active site of the enzyme, a .... is released. The enzyme

remains unchanged and continues catalysing reactions. Enzymes work best at

certain conditions of pH and .... The ideal pH (when the reaction

occurs at the fastest possible rate) is known as the .... pH, and the

ideal temperature is known as the optimum temperature. If the temperature or pH

is too high, the enzyme will lose its shape and is said to be ....

Exercise 5.2 Effect of temperature on enzymes

IN THIS EXERCISE YOU WILL:

Science skills:

- interpret information about enzymes from a graph.

English skills:

- use scientific words to write more effectively.

KEY WORDS

kinetic energy: energy of moving objects

The effect of pH and temperature on enzymes is often demonstrated in a graph.

You need to be able to observe what is happening in a graph, and to draw logical conclusions from this that come from your scientific knowledge.

When describing what happens in a graph, try to include as much information as possible.

LANGUAGE FOCUS

Selecting the correct word is a skill that allows you to explain scientifically what is happening during the use of enzymes. For example, denature is the scientific word for *stop functioning*; *increase* is one of the scientific words for *go up*.

Look at these examples:

A   The rate of reaction went up as the temperature went up.

B   The rate of reaction increased as the temperature increased.

Notice how sentence B uses the word *increased*. The style of sentence B is more scientific and formal. Generally speaking, common multi-word verbs like *go up, go down, look at, write down*, which are frequent in conversation are substituted in scientific writing with single-word verbs like *increase, decrease, observe, record.*

C   The enzyme denatured at 38 °C.

D   The enzyme stopped working at 38 °C.

In this example, sentence C uses the word *denatured*. This is much better and more scientific than answer D. It is a specialised word which shows that you understand the topic and that you write like a scientist.

LANGUAGE TIP

Remember that *effect* is almost always used as a noun in biology and *affect* as a verb – try not to confuse them. *Affect* comes first alphabetically, and an action *to affect* has to happen before you can have a result (*effect*).

Figure 5.2 shows how temperature affects the rate of reaction of an enzyme.

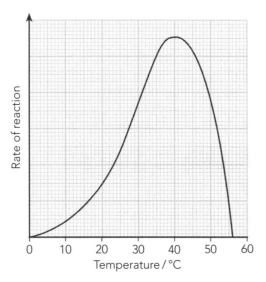

Figure 5.2: The effect of temperature on the rate of reaction of an enzyme.

2   Use the graph to write a sentence that includes the scientific words or phrases given. Your sentence should include data where necessary.

For example:

'rate of reaction is increasing'

The rate of reaction is increasing from 0 °C to 40 °C.

a   'optimum temperature'

    ....

    ....

b   'begins to denature'

    ....

    ....

c   'is completely denatured'

    ....

    ....

d   'the rate of reaction decreases because'

    ....

    ....

    ....

e 'the molecules have more **kinetic energy**'

....

....

....

Exercise 5.3 Using enzymes in industry

IN THIS EXERCISE YOU WILL:

Science skills:

- learn about how enzymes are used in industry.

English skills:

- practise the skill of extracting information from a section of text and use phrases *such as*, *for instance* and *including*.

KEY WORD

catalyst: a substance that increases the rate of a chemical reaction and is not changed by the reaction.

Enzymes are used in industry because the enzymes can be used to control and speed up reactions that are useful. This allows companies to make their products work faster and better, which is good for people who use them.

Read the following text:

Enzymes are biological **catalysts** that work best in their optimum conditions of pressure, temperature and pH. Enzymes are used commercially in many different ways, such as in creating washing powder.

Pharmaceutical companies use catalase to speed up the healing of wounds. Catalase converts hydrogen peroxide to oxygen and water.

Clothing, such as leather, is softened by using a specific protease. Stains can also be removed by enzymes: fats can be removed from clothing by adding lipases to washing powders. The fats are broken down into fatty acids and glycerol. This same method can be applied to use proteases to break down and remove proteins from clothing.

Isomerase converts glucose to fructose to add a sweeter taste to some foods. Pectinase can be used to extract fruit juices for human consumption. Even babies can benefit from enzymes, as proteases are added to formula milk to make digestion easier.

LANGUAGE TIP

In biology, you often have to read long texts and extract important information from them.
Try these techniques to help you:

- Highlight or underline key words and phrases.

- Use different coloured pens to highlight information that is relevant in different ways (for example, green for causes, blue for effects).

Answer the following questions based on the passage.

3   Write down the names of the five enzymes that are mentioned in the text.

....

....

4   **a**   What is the substrate that pharmaceutical companies target with catalase?

....

   b   What is the substrate in question **4a** broken down into?

....

5   What are lipids broken down into by lipase?

....

6   How might lipase and protease be denatured when washing clothes?

....

....

....

....

LANGUAGE FOCUS

To talk about examples of something, as well as *for example*, we use the phrases *such as, for instance,* and *including*.

Enzymes, *such as* amylase and protease, have specific shapes.

Some enzymes, *for instance* pepsin, can work at a very low pH.

Enzymes, *including* lipase, are released from glands.

7   Write a sentence from the text about enzymes that uses an example.

....

....

8   Write a sentence of your own that includes an example of a type of enzyme.
   You may use the information in the Language Focus box to help if you wish,
   but write your own version.

....

....

Plant nutrition

Science skills:

- compare organic and inorganic molecules

- describe structure and function of parts of a plant

- describe and explain a graph to show how limiting factors affect growth of plants.

English skills:

- write sentences to link causes with effects.

Exercise 6.1 Inorganic to organic

IN THIS EXERCISE YOU WILL:

Science skills:

- compare organic and inorganic molecules.

English skills:

- identify the meaning of words that contain the prefixes in- and im-.

The words organic and inorganic have different meanings in biology and everyday life. As a biologist, it is important that you have a clear idea what these terms mean, and how to use them. Substances are either organic or inorganic.

1   Write the headings 'Organic' and 'Inorganic' in the correct place in the table.

....	....
contains both carbon and hydrogen, as well as other molecules	does not contain carbon and hydrogen
produced by living organisms	used by living organisms to build more complex materials

> You do not need to know any details of the term inorganic, as it is beyond the requirements of the syllabus.

2   These substances are all related to plant nutrition. Place them into the table below to show whether each substance is *inorganic* or *organic*.

carbohydrates   carbon dioxide   glucose   magnesium

oxygen   proteins   starch   water

Organic substances	Inorganic substances
....	....
....	....
....	....
....	....

3   For each of these terms, state the meaning of the word.

a   inactive: ....

b   independent: ....

c   imperfect: ....

LANGUAGE TIP

The prefixes *in-* and *im-* mean 'not'. When you see them at the start of an adjective, you can easily work out the meaning. Look:

impossible = not possible

impractical = not practical

incorrect = not correct

Exercise 6.2 Limiting factors

IN THIS EXERCISE YOU WILL:

Science skills:

* use a graph to understand how limiting factors affect growth of plants.

English skills:

* select the appropriate terms for describing and explaining patterns in a graph.

KEY WORDS

limiting factor: a factor that is in short supply, which stops an activity (such as photosynthesis) happening at a faster rate

photosynthesis: the process by which plants synthesise carbohydrates from raw materials using energy from light

A graph that shows the rate of **photosynthesis** is useful for observing how different conditions can affect the rate. In this exercise, you will practise describing a graph, and writing about photosynthesis.

Sometimes the amount of sunlight, the concentration of carbon dioxide and the temperature might be ideal for photosynthesis. If one of these is not ideal, then this will be the **limiting factor** of photosynthesis. A limiting factor is something (such as the amount of light available) that limits the growth of the plant.

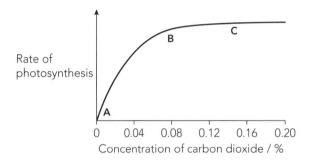

Figure 6.1: How the concentration of carbon dioxide affects the rate of photosynthesis.

Look at the sentences below about Figure 6.1. The first sentence is about the gradient of the graph (how steep the graph is). The second statement is about what the graph tells us.

In section A, the gradient of the graph is steep.

This shows that the rate of photosynthesis is increasing rapidly.

LANGUAGE FOCUS

In science, you often need to be able to describe a graph. In order to do this, you need specific vocabulary. Features of a graph include:

- axis/axes (x-axis, y-axis)

- gradient

- curve

- line

- point

- origin

- intersect.

You also need to explain what is happening when the shape of a graph changes. These words will help you describe the patterns and changes that you see in a graph:

less steep	steeper	increasing	decreasing	horizontal
	vertical	constant	changing	

4   Label the graph using the features of a graph listed in the Language Focus box.

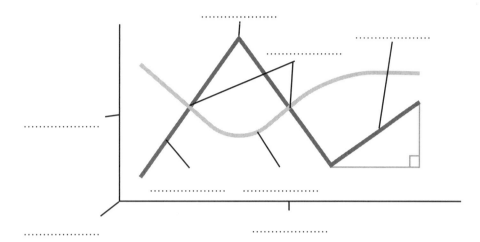

For questions **5** and **6**, use words from the Language Focus box to describe and explain the changes in Figure 6.1. You do not need to use all of the words.

5   How does the graph change in section B?

In section B, the gradient of the graph is ....

This shows that the rate of photosynthesis is ....

6   Describe and explain the graph in section C.

In section C, the gradient of the graph is ....

This shows that the rate of photosynthesis is ....

The next two questions require you to use the data in Figure 6.1.

7   What is the concentration of carbon dioxide when the rate of photosynthesis begins to slow down? ....

8   What is the limiting factor for this particular plant? ....

Exercise 6.3 Mineral ion deficiencies in plants

IN THIS EXERCISE YOU WILL:

Science skills:

- explain the appearance of healthy and unhealthy plants.

English skills:

- express a conclusion from an observation made.

KEY WORD

symptoms: features that you experience when you have a disease

Plants take in mineral ions from the soil to allow them to make proteins and other substances that are vital for growth and good health. These mineral ions include:

- nitrates
- phosphates
- potassium
- magnesium.

If the plant does not get enough of these mineral ions, it will not grow as well or as healthily as a plant that does. The signs of an unhealthy plant are known as **symptoms** and you can use these to work out which mineral ions a plant is lacking (see Table 6.1).

Mineral ion	Symptoms of mineral ion deficiency
nitrates	lower leaves are yellow or dead, upper leaves are pale green
potassium	poor flower and fruit growth, yellow leaves with dead spots
phosphates	purple leaves and small roots
magnesium	lower leaves turn yellow

Table 6.1: Mineral ion deficiencies in plants.

LANGUAGE FOCUS

Look at these sentences:

This plant looks healthy. Therefore, it must be getting everything it needs.

'This plant looks healthy' is an observation – something you can see. 'The plant is getting everything it needs' is something you can conclude from the observation – that it is healthy.

We can use words to connect a conclusion to an observation. To express a conclusion, you can either:

- start a new sentence with *Therefore* or *Consequently*:
  This plant looks healthy. *Consequently*, it must be getting everything it needs.
  The plant has yellow leaves. *Therefore*, the plant must have a nitrate deficiency.

- continue the same sentence with *so* or *which suggests*:
  This plant looks healthy, *which suggests* it must be getting everything it needs.
  This plant looks healthy, *so* it must be getting everything it needs.

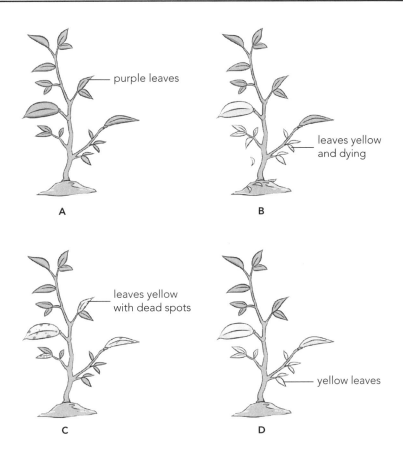

Figure 6.2: Plants with mineral ion deficiencies.

Use Table 6.1 to decide what each plant shown in Figure 6.2 is deficient in. Complete the sentences to link your conclusions to the correct symptoms.

Here is an example to help you:

Plant A has purple leaves. Therefore, it must be deficient in phosphates.

9   Plant B ....

Therefore, it must be deficient in ....

10   Plant C ...., which suggests ....

....

11   Now write the two whole sentences for Plant D.

....

....

Exercise 6.4 Words to describe plants

IN THIS EXERCISE YOU WILL:

Science skills:

- describe the structure and function of the parts of a plant.

English skills:

- use common English words to express complicated biological concepts.

LANGUAGE TIP

Some words in English can be used as more than one grammatical type of word. For example, transport, guard and limit can be verbs and nouns. Look at the other words in the sentence to help you decide if they are working as verbs or not.

This limits it. (verb)
There are limits. (noun)

It is possible to use everyday words to help biological understanding. One example of this is describing a leaf as a food factory. A factory is a place where things are made. A leaf uses raw materials to 'make' food for distribution around the plant.

12 Here are eight words connected with plants. The table below contains eight definitions. Write each word in the correct space in the table. The first one has been done for you.

'v' means that the term is a verb, 'n' a noun and 'adj' an adjective.

absorb (v)   factory (n)   guard (v)   limit (v, n)   release (v)

simple (adj)   transport (v)   vessel (n)

	Word	Meaning	Relation to plants	Extra information
a	factory	where goods are made	a leaf uses raw materials	food for distribution
b	....	take in or soak up	water is taken in at roots	for instance, roots …
c	....	allow to escape	the products of photosynthesis	for example, oxygen produced through photosynthesis is given out
d	....	made of a single or very few elements	sugars such as glucose	the opposite of complex
e	....	carry from place to another	water, mineral ions and sugars	movement of compounds
f	....	control	cells at a stoma	control the amount of carbon dioxide
g	....	a hollow container	xylem and phloem	transport water and mineral ions
h	....	sets a limit to	carbon dioxide, water and sunlight	… the rate of photosynthesis

13 Now use the information from the table above to write sentences about plants. Use the word, its meaning and how it is related to plants in your sentences. Here is an example to help you:

factory / make: A factory is a place where goods are made. A leaf uses raw materials to 'make' food for distribution around the plant.

a   guard / protect

....

....

....

b   vessel / transports

....

....

....

c   absorb / take in

....

....

....

d   release / escape

....

....

....

e   transport / to move

....

....

....

f   limit / cannot increase

....

....

....

g   simple / cannot be broken down

....

....

....

> **LANGUAGE TIP**
>
> Be prepared for common English words to appear in biological texts that have a specific biological meaning. Think about what they mean in general English; it might unlock what they do in biology.

Human nutrition

Science skills:

- apply knowledge of a balanced diet.

English skills:

- explain the role of enzymes in digestion using the present simple passive

- identify the digestive organs and outline key stages of digestion using correct verb or noun forms.

Exercise 7.1 Recommending a balanced diet

IN THIS EXERCISE YOU WILL:

Science skills:

- recommend a balanced diet.

English skills:

- meet and practise *fewer* and *less* with countable and uncountable nouns, and verbs.

> **KEY WORDS**
>
> **balanced diet:** a diet that contains all of the required nutrients, in suitable proportions, and the right amount of energy

> **LANGUAGE TIP**
>
> Remember: *advice* is a noun; *advise* is a verb. When we give our friends advice, we advise them.

A **balanced diet** allows the body to grow and develop in a healthy manner.

Sometimes, it is important to offer advice about how a person could eat more or less of a particular food group.

LANGUAGE FOCUS

There are some things that you can count, such as plants, vegetables or leaves (one plant, two plants, three plants, etc.). There are also things that you cannot count, such as oxygen, water or air (we would not say 'one oxygen, two oxygens', etc.).

To talk about higher amounts, you can use *more* with countable things (plants, leaves) and with uncountable things (oxygen, air). *You need more vegetables. You need more fresh air.*

To talk about lower amounts, you can use *fewer* with countable things, but use *less* with uncountable things:

You should watch fewer videos.

You should eat less red meat.

You can also use *more* and *less* after verbs:

You should go outside more.

You should eat less.

Remember: *more* and *less* go before nouns and adjectives, but after verbs.

Read the information then do the task below.

Arun has decided to monitor his diet, because he wants to be healthier. He has made a list of what he ate on one school day, so that his friend Sofia can help him work out if his diet is balanced or not.

Breakfast	Lunch	Dinner
Cereal	Cheeseburger	Fish and rice
Toast with butter and jam	French fries	Ice cream
Cup of tea with three sugars	Chicken wings	Bottle of cola
Glass of orange juice	Large piece of chocolate cake	Glass of water
	Packet of crisps	
	Bottle of cola	

Sofia looks at Arun's diet and gives him advice.

1   Read the sentences and circle the correct option to complete Sofia's advice.

Arun, your diet gives you a lot of energy but you should eat **more / less** chocolate, cake, and ice cream, and **more / fewer** crisps, or you will become obese. These are fatty foods.

There are no vegetables in your diet, so you should eat **more / fewer** of these, to make sure that you get plenty of mineral ions.

You have three sugars in your tea! I think that you should definitely have **more / less** sugar in your tea. In fact, I suggest you need **more / less** water in your diet, too.

You get vitamin C from the orange juice, but maybe if you drink **more / fewer / less** fizzy drinks, it would be better for you.

It's OK to have chocolate cake sometimes, but when you eat so many fats in one day, you should definitely try having **more / less** – maybe just a small piece.

You have plenty of carbohydrates from the bread, rice and potatoes. The meat and the fish supply the correct proportion of protein, but please eat **fewer / more** vegetables and **fewer / more** fats.

<table>
<tr><td>LANGUAGE TIP</td></tr>
<tr><td>Try using *plenty of* to mean 'a good amount of'. It is similar to *a lot of*, but often has a positive meaning:

Lydia doesn't eat much fruit, but she eats plenty of vegetables and salad.</td></tr>
</table>

Exercise 7.2 Digestive enzymes

IN THIS EXERCISE YOU WILL:

Science skills:

- explain the role of digestive enzymes.

English skills:

- practise the passive voice.

Carbohydrates and fats must be broken down so that they can be used to release the energy that the body requires. Proteins are digested and help our bodies to grow and repair.

2 The word string below contains some key words related to the digestion of carbohydrates, fats and proteins. Separate the words and write them on the lines below.

carbohydratesfatsproteinsfattyacidsaminoacidsglycerollipaseproteasecarbohydraseglucose

....

....

....

....

3 Use your knowledge to insert the names of three digestive enzymes from the word string into the table.

Nutrient	Digestive enzyme	Product
carbohydrates	....	simple sugars
fats/lipids	....	fatty acids and glycerol
proteins	....	amino acids

<table>
<tr><td>LANGUAGE TIP</td></tr>
<tr><td>The name of the digestive enzyme is usually similar to the nutrient that it breaks down. Carbohydrates are broken down by carbohydrase – both words begin with 'carbohydr'. However, carbohydrates are broken down by a carbohydrase called *amylase*. You are expected to use amylase when referring to the enzyme that breaks down carbohydrates.</td></tr>
</table>

4   Now that you have the information about the enzymes used in digestion, put them into sentences. Here is an example:

Carbohydrates are broken down by amylases to produce simple sugars.

LANGUAGE FOCUS

As we saw in Chapter 4, this sentence is passive. In this case it is the present simple passive and describes a fact.

We start the sentence with the main term we want to define:	*Carbohydrates*
Choose the correct form of the verb to be (is or are):	*are*
Add the past participle – the third form of the verb:	*broken down*
Add 'by' and the enzyme:	*by amylases.*

In definitions or statements where the enzyme is important or less obvious, use *by* + enzyme:

Carbohydrates are broken down by amylases.

Chocolate is kept in a runny state by invertase.

Now write sentences for the other two examples in the table.

a   Fats/lipids:

....

....

b   Proteins:

....

....

Exercise 7.3 Digestion key words

IN THIS EXERCISE YOU WILL:

Science skills:

* outline key stages of digestion.

English skills:

* know the difference between noun and verb forms.

KEY WORD

digestion: the process of breaking down large, insoluble molecules into smaller, soluble molecules

---

Digestion is a topic that will introduce you to a series of new words and names for parts of the body. Many words in this topic come from the same word families, and it is important for you to select the correct word for the appropriate sentence. This exercise will help you to select the correct word and use it where suitable.

LANGUAGE FOCUS

Many words have different forms which we use in different ways in sentences.

When you describe actions or states, you use a verb. For example, *to react*:

Different chemicals react with each other in our bodies.

The names of the processes taking place are nouns. For example:

When proteases break down proteins, this is a chemical reaction.

Nouns expressing processes often end in *-ion*, and this is true of many words connected with digestion. To form the noun from the verb you can use verb + *ion*:

react – reaction   *digest – digestion*

---

5   The sentences define some key words related to digestion. Circle the correct verb or noun to complete each sentence.

   a   **Ingestion / Ingest** is when food and drink substances are taken into the body through the mouth.

   b   The breaking down of large, insoluble molecules into small, soluble molecules is **digestion / digest**.

   c   Molecules are **absorbed / absorption** through the wall of the alimentary canal.

   d   Digested food molecules are **assimilation / assimilated** to the parts of the body where they are required.

   e   Undigested food molecules are **egested / egestion** through the anus.

   f   Muscles **contract / contraction** and relax to help food move along some parts of the alimentary canal.

   g   **Deaminate / Deamination** is when the nitrogen part of amino acids is removed and occurs in the liver.

Exercise 7.4 The journey of digestion

IN THIS EXERCISE YOU WILL:

Science skills:

* identify the digestive organs.

English skills:

* write a description of the process of digestion

KEY WORDS

alimentary canal: the part of the digestive system through which food passes as it moves from the mouth to the anus

The molecules are broken down through a series of processes in the **alimentary canal** and with help from other digestive organs.

6 Below is a list of digestive organs. Use each word to label the diagram.

large intestine   mouth   anus   stomach   rectum

oesophagus   pancreas   liver   small intestine

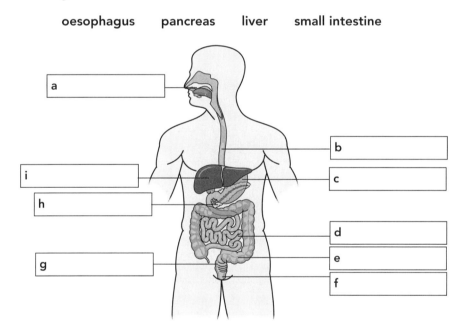

7   Write an exciting story about the journey of a piece of food from when it is eaten to when it is removed from the body. You must include:

- the names of all the organs that the food passes through using the diagram above to help you

- information about enzymes and conditions in the body (amylase, lipase and protease)

- names and characters to make your story as interesting as possible

- any other scientific content that is important in digestion, such as the role of the liver and pancreas in the digestion of food.

Here is an example of how the story could begin:

Zara looked at her chicken and rice and thought about the journey it was going to take. Zara put Riya Rice into her mouth, where Riya met her friend Sarita Saliva. Sarita Saliva had many enzymes to help break down Riya Rice into smaller pieces so Zara could swallow her. Riya was very happy as she went down the oesophagus towards the stomach. But she quickly got scared, because the stomach was dark and acidic. Luckily, she escaped into the small intestine where she was…

LANGUAGE TIP
To make a story exciting, try using adverbs such as *suddenly*, *luckily*, *sadly* and expressions of time, like *just then*, *very soon*, *not long after*, *at that moment*, *after a long* (journey), etc. You can also add expressions like *What a surprise! What a shock! What fun! What a fright!*

....

....

....

....

....

....

....

....

....

....

....

....

....

....

....

....

> Chapter 8
Transport in plants

IN THIS CHAPTER YOU WILL:

Science skills:

- identify and compare key words for transport in plants.

English skills:

- use linkers to describe the structure and function of vessels in plant transport

- use the first conditional to explain what happens to plants in certain conditions.

Exercise 8.1 Key words in plant transport

IN THIS EXERCISE YOU WILL:

Science skills:

- identify the key words for transport in plants.

English skills:

- recognise key words in a longer piece of text.

KEY WORDS

lignin: a hard, strong, waterproof substance that forms the walls of xylem vessels

phloem: a plant tissue made up of living cells joined end to end; it transports substances made by the plant, such as sucrose and amino acids

vascular bundles: collections of xylem tubes and phloem vessels running side by side, which form the veins in a leaf

xylem: a plant tissue made up of dead, empty cells joined end to end; it transports water and mineral ions and helps to support the plant

Read the passage, which highlights some of the key structures and functions of the xylem and the phloem.

This exercise will help you to learn the differences and similarities between two important vessels in plants – **xylem** and **phloem**. You will need to focus on identifying the key words to complete this section.

Plants take in most of their water, mineral ions and nutrients from the soil and must transfer these to all of the different parts of the plant where they will be required.

The two main vessels of transport – the xylem and the phloem – are responsible for this, but have different structures and functions.

The xylem is made up of hollow, dead cells to form hollow tubes. These vessels transport water and mineral ions in one direction from the roots to the leaves. The walls of xylem vessels contain **lignin**, which keeps the plant upright due to the strength of lignin.

Phloem vessels have sieve plates to allow them to carry the nutrients made by the plant to where they are needed. As they could be needed at any part of the plant, phloem vessels are able to carry nutrients in both directions.

Xylem and phloem vessels are usually found together in **vascular bundles**.

1 The word search contains 11 key words and phrases from the passage about xylem and phloem. Find these words/phrases in any direction and circle them on the word search.

X	V	V	A	S	C	U	L	A	R	S	O
Y	B	E	R	I	A	C	I	S	B	W	N
L	H	S	Z	E	W	E	G	V	A	W	E
E	A	S	X	V	B	R	N	R	W	A	D
M	A	E	G	E	U	T	I	R	B	T	I
E	V	L	B	T	B	U	N	D	L	E	R
J	U	S	E	F	M	M	L	O	O	R	E
M	I	N	E	R	A	L	A	R	T	U	C
P	R	L	B	O	O	M	E	R	S	T	T
R	E	N	U	T	R	I	E	N	T	S	I
V	C	Q	C	V	G	W	A	T	G	U	O
P	H	L	O	E	M	W	T	U	O	D	N

LANGUAGE TIP

To help remember that xylem moves water up and phloem moves substances down through the plant: remember that *xy* (xylem) goes high but *phlo* (phloem) goes low. Say the sentence out loud to help you remember.

2   Some of the words from the previous question relate to the xylem, to the phloem, or to both of the vessels. List the words that you found in the correct column of the table. One of the boxes has been completed for you.

Xylem	Phloem	Both vessels
one direction	....	....
....	....	....
....	....	....

Exercise 8.2 Linking structure to function

IN THIS EXERCISE YOU WILL:

Science skills:

*   link the structure and function of vessels in plant transport.

English skills:

*   use linkers to combine two different points.

In order to demonstrate your understanding of how vessel structure is linked to its function, you need to be able to link the structure and the function together into one sentence.

LANGUAGE FOCUS

When we want to link a cause with its effect, we can use the words *so* and *because*. Sometimes, we might use *consequently*.

Consequently and *so* go at the start of the *effect* part of the sentence.

Because goes at the start of the *cause* part of the sentence.

cause   **effect**
Arteries have a small lumen, *so* blood is pumped at high pressure.

           effect   **cause**
Greenhouse gases are released into the atmosphere, *because* fossil fuels are burned.

cause   **effect**
Sunlight is a stimulus for plant growth. *Consequently*, it causes plants to grow towards the light.

Notice where the commas or full stops go.

3 Use the words from Exercise 8.1 to write your own paragraph about the structure and function of the plant transport vessels. You should explain:

   • how the structure supports the plant

   • how the structure relates to the function.

   You should use the sentence structure from the Language Focus box to make your sentences clear.

   a xylem

   ....

   ....

   ....

   ....

   ....

   b phloem

   ....

   ....

   ....

   ....

   ....

Exercise 8.3 Explaining the effect of conditions on plants

IN THIS EXERCISE YOU WILL:

Science skills:

- explain what happens to plants in certain conditions.

English skills:

- use the first conditional when explaining what happens to plants in certain conditions.

Temperature, wind speed and humidity can affect a plant. You can use the first conditional to link the action to the consequence, or the cause to the effect.

LANGUAGE FOCUS

In science, the first conditional is often used for predictions. For example:

If you burn coal, you will pollute the atmosphere.

If more weights are added, the spring will extend further.

If we remove weights, the spring will not extend further.

We form it like this:

If + present simple, subject + will (not) + verb

We can also substitute *will* with *can, could, should, might* and *may* in first conditional sentences. Using these verbs makes the prediction less certain, or less probable than with *will*:

If too many weights are added, the spring *might break*. (= a possibility)

Notice that you can also put the part of the sentence with *if* second:

The spring *might break if* too many weights are added.

You *will pollute* the atmosphere *if* you burn coal.

4   For each of the examples below, write your own sentences using the first conditional to make predictions about a plant.

  a   If the temperature is too high, the plant will

       ....

  b   If the wind speed is fast, the plant will

       ....

  c   If the humidity is very low, most plants will

       ....

Chapter 9

Transport in animals

IN THIS CHAPTER YOU WILL:

Science skills:

- describe how materials are transported within animals and the structure and function of the human circulatory system

- understand the effects of an unhealthy lifestyle

- explain the effect of exercise on human heart rate.

English skills:

- use *this* when referring to a pronoun and prepositions to describe a function.

Exercise 9.1 Oxygen in the blood

IN THIS EXERCISE YOU WILL:

Science skills:

- identify key words associated with the circulatory system.

English skills:

- use *this* when referring to a pronoun.

KEY WORDS

circulatory system: a system of blood vessels with a pump and valves to ensure one-way flow of blood

It is essential that oxygen is moved around the body to allow organs and cells to release energy as part of the respiration process.

1   Circle the word *this* in the text (there are four). Then underline the words or facts
    that *this* refers to.

> The **circulatory system** of mammals is a network of vessels and organs
> that allow blood to flow around the body. This network is how substanc-
> es such as oxygen, glucose, carbon dioxide and urea are moved around
> the body to where they are needed. This system depends on a central
> pump – the heart. The heart pumps the blood around the body, using the
> large network of blood vessels. Blood that does not carry oxygen leaves
> the heart and travels to the lungs. There, the blood collects oxygen. This
> oxygen then goes to the left-hand side of the heart, and is then pumped all
> around the body. The blood delivers the oxygen to the cells that need it,
> and then returns to the heart again. In humans, this happens around three
> times per minute.

LANGUAGE FOCUS

We use the word 'this' to refer to things that are 'near' us. We can use it to
refer to singular objects, for example in our hands (this book), or things we are
working with at the present time (this exercise). In a paragraph, 'this' refers to
something near it in the text. For example:

An experiment is carried out to measure the effects of exercise on the heart.
This experiment is carried out using a static bicycle.

This indicates the experiment in the sentence before.

His heart beats at a rate of 60 beats per minute. This means he has a
healthy heart.

This refers to the nearest fact to the word *this*, in this case the rate of
the heartbeat.

The plural form is *these*.

2   Read the text in question **1** again. Write the key terms referred to by *this* in the
    table below.

	Key term	Meaning
a	....	*This* is where the blood collects oxygen.
b	....	Blood is pumped all around *this* by the heart.
c	....	*This* substance is carried around the body in the blood.
d	....	*This* is the network of vessels and organs that pass blood around the body.
e	....	*This* is the central pump of the body.

3 Below is a diagram of the heart. Complete the labels using the words from the word string.

rightventricletobodytolungsfromlungsleftatrium

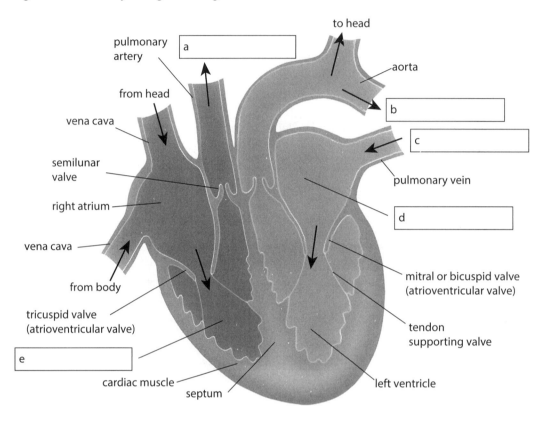

pulmonary artery

a

to head

from head

aorta

vena cava

b

c

semilunar valve

pulmonary vein

right atrium

d

vena cava

mitral or bicuspid valve (atrioventricular valve)

from body

tricuspid valve (atrioventricular valve)

tendon supporting valve

e

cardiac muscle

left ventricle

septum

LANGUAGE TIP

Remember the order that blood passes through the chambers of the heart is A–V (atrium – ventricle), in alphabetical order. The valve between the chambers is often referred to as the atrioventricular valve (AV).

Exercise 9.2 Taking care of your heart

IN THIS EXERCISE YOU WILL:

Science skills:

* link unhealthy lifestyle to common heart diseases.

English skills:

* complete sentences about the effect of unhealthy lifestyles.

KEY WORDS

coronary heart disease (CHD): disease caused by blockage of the coronary arteries

The causes of **coronary heart disease (CHD)** are well known, and there are lots of things that a person can do to reduce the risk of coronary heart disease.

4   Write the letters in the correct order to find the names of factors that increase the risk of heart disease.

    a   SMOGINK   ....

    b   BITESOY   ....

    c   TIED   ....

    d   RESTSS   ....

    e   ICEGENTS   ....

5   Arun's father has recently been to the doctor and admitted that he occasionally smokes cigarettes. Although he exercises regularly, Arun's father eats a lot of chocolate and other fatty foods. The doctor gave Arun's father some advice to reduce the risk of getting coronary heart disease.

    Complete these two sentences that the doctor might have said to Arun's father for him to live a healthier and longer life.

    a   Arun's father should .... when he is stressed.

    b   Arun's father should .... his diet.

6   What does Arun's father do often that will reduce the risk of heart disease? Complete this sentence:

    Arun's father often ....

LANGUAGE FOCUS

When we talk about or give advice, we often use *should, ought to* and *X is good for you* to say that something is a good idea and is recommendable.

You should get regular exercise to keep your heart healthy.

You ought to sleep around eight hours a day.

Laughing is good for you.

To say that something is a bad idea and to advise against things, we often use *shouldn't* and *Y is bad for you.*

You shouldn't eat too many doughnuts and other fatty foods.

Sitting in front of a screen all day is bad for you.

Note: *oughtn't* (*ought not*) exists, but is rarely used.

Put the verb that expresses the recommendation after *should* and *ought to.*

Put a noun or *-ing* form that expresses the recommendation before *is good/ bad for you.*

You should/ought to get regular exercise.

Getting regular exercise is good for you.

7   Complete the sentences below to give advice on how to be healthy.

    a   should / shouldn't

        You .... eat lots of chocolate every day.

    b   ought to / shouldn't

        You .... eat plenty of vegetables every day.

    c   is / isn't

        Watching television all day .... a good idea.

    d   is good / isn't good

        Having a balanced diet .... for your health.

LANGUAGE TIP

Some verbs need 'to' after them, when you add another verb (*want to try, need to go, have to get, ought to eat,* etc.), but *should* never needs 'to'. Remember, it works exactly the same way as *would, can, will, could* and *might.*

Exercise 9.3 Blood vessels

IN THIS EXERCISE YOU WILL:

Science skills:

*   explain how different blood vessels ensure that blood flows freely.

English skills:

*   use prepositions to describe a function of blood vessels.

KEY WORDS

artery: a thick-walled vessel that takes high-pressure blood away from the heart

capillary: a tiny vessel with walls only one cell thick, that takes blood close to body cells

vein: a thin-walled vessel that takes low-pressure blood back to the heart

Describing what happens to the blood as it passes through blood vessels requires the use of prepositions. This exercise will guide you through how the blood travels around the body and the prepositions that help you to describe the direction that the blood travels.

8   Look at the diagrams showing an **artery**, a **capillary**, and a **vein** and choose the missing word for each of the boxes labelled **a–f** using the list of words provided.

lumen   muscles   smooth   thick   thin   very small

An artery

thick outer wall

b lining

small lumen

a layer of muscles and elastic fibres

A capillary

c lumen

wall made of a single layer of cells

A vein

fairly **d** outer wall

smooth lining

thin layer of **f** and elastic fibres

large **e**

a   ....

b   ....

c   ....

d   ....

e   ....

f   ....

The structure of each of these vessels depends on their function. The vessels that carry blood a long distance need to have very strong walls because of the high pressure of the blood when it leaves the heart. The blood flowing back to the heart can be easily pushed along wide vessels by contracting muscles.

LANGUAGE FOCUS

On, in, next to, into, at, in front of, behind, under and *opposite* are all prepositions. Prepositions often tell us about time (on Monday), place (at school) or movement/direction (up the hill). Sometimes the 'movement' can be real or imagined; for example, *put into* (groups / categories), *divide into* (sections), *separate into* (types), *categorise under* (headings) etc.

In question **9** you will use prepositions that show direction.

9 Each vessel carries blood in a certain direction. Complete the text by writing the correct preposition in the gaps.

away   into   out   to   towards

Arteries carry blood .... from the heart and .... the cells of

the body at high pressure. Arteries divide .... smaller vessels until they

are capillaries. Capillaries take blood .... the cells and organs and allow

the nutrients and oxygen to diffuse .... The capillaries join together

again to form veins. Veins allow blood to travel .... from the cells and

back .... the heart.

LANGUAGE TIP

<u>A</u>rteries carry blood <u>a</u>way from the heart. Ve<u>ins</u> carry blood <u>in</u>to the heart.

Ⓐrtery   Veⓘn

Ⓐway   ⓘnto

Exercise 9.4 Effect of exercise on heart rate

IN THIS EXERCISE YOU WILL:

Science skills:

- describe and explain what happens to the heart rate during exercise.

English skills:

- understand the command terms *describe* and *explain*, to identify the depth of the answer required.

LANGUAGE FOCUS

In Chapter 3 there is a discussion of the command words *describe* and *explain*. You are going to practise these terms here. Look back at the explanation in Chapter 3 if you are not sure about what these words ask you to do.

Remember that command terms use imperatives. Imperatives are verbs used to give instructions, orders or commands. For example:

Measure the amount of carbon dioxide produced.

Evaluate how well you did the experiment.

Calculate your body mass index.

Look at the graph below and complete the exercise that follows. Figure 9.1 shows the heart rate of a man before, during and after exercise.

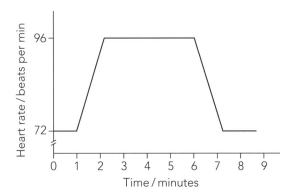

Figure 9.1: Graph to show the heart rate of a man before, during and after exercise.

10 The following table contains statements. These statements either describe or explain what is happening in Figure 9.1. Tick the correct box for each statement. The first one has been completed for you.

	Statement	Describe	Explain
a	The man has stopped exercising after six minutes.	✓	
b	The heart rate is increasing from one minute up to two minutes.		
c	The heart is now beginning to pump blood faster around the body.		
d	The heart rate has stopped increasing at this point (after two minutes).		
e	The heart rate after one minute is 72 beats per minute.		
f	The heart rate is increasing from 72 beats per minute to 96 beats per minute.		
g	The man has completed his exercise and so the heart begins to pump less blood around the body.		
h	The heart rate has returned to its normal resting rate.		

11 Here is an example, using a description and an explanation.

Description: Marcus's breathing rate increased rapidly after three minutes.

Explanation: Marcus's breathing rate increased because his muscles were using up oxygen for respiration and he needed to take more oxygen into his body.

Combined sentence:

Marcus's breathing rate increased rapidly after three minutes because his muscles were using up oxygen for respiration and he needed to take more oxygen into his body.

Combine descriptions and explanations from the table in question **10** to write a sentence that describes and explains what has happened.

....

....

....

....

Chapter 10

Diseases and immunity

> **IN THIS CHAPTER YOU WILL:**
>
> Science skills:
>
> - understand how the body protects itself from disease and infection
>
> - understand how the body is affected by cholera.
>
> English skills:
>
> - use comparisons to aid your understanding of the immune system.

Exercise 10.1 Key words in diseases and immunity

> **IN THIS EXERCISE YOU WILL:**
>
> Science skills:
>
> - understand how the body fights against disease.
>
> English skills:
>
> - construct sentences about key words.

> **KEY WORDS**
>
> **active immunity:** long-term defence against a pathogen by antibody production in the body
>
> **antibiotic:** a substance that is taken into the body, and which kills bacteria but does not affect human cells or viruses
>
> **antibodies:** molecules secreted by white blood cells, which bind to pathogens and help to destroy them
>
> **antigen:** a chemical that is recognised by the body as being 'foreign' – that is, it is not part of the body's normal set of chemical substances – and stimulates the production of antibodies
>
> **passive immunity:** short-term defence against a pathogen by antibodies acquired from another individual, such as from mother to infant
>
> **pathogens:** microorganisms that cause disease, such as bacteria
>
> **transmissible disease:** a disease that can be passed from one host to another; transmissible diseases are caused by pathogens

It is important to be able to identify the key words associated with diseases and immunity.

1 Find and circle 14 different key terms from the diseases and immunity topic in the word search. The terms can be forwards, backwards or diagonal.

active   antibiotics   antibody   antigen   cholera

defences   diseases   immunity   memory   MRSA

passive   pathogen   transmissible   vaccination

A	F	A	R	U	V	U	B	I	D	D	H	D	Z	I
D	I	S	E	A	S	E	S	Y	P	E	I	E	M	L
N	T	B	W	S	K	B	X	D	A	F	F	M	J	U
B	E	R	B	K	I	K	M	O	S	E	U	O	F	C
J	A	G	A	W	Z	B	Y	B	S	N	Y	W	W	N
W	Z	I	I	N	R	L	L	I	I	C	Z	J	E	R
T	Z	H	U	T	S	Y	E	T	V	E	I	G	G	M
T	D	C	B	V	N	M	Y	N	E	S	O	O	E	A
E	V	I	T	C	A	A	I	A	E	H	A	M	R	Q
N	S	S	O	C	N	I	M	S	T	H	O	Y	E	A
T	O	N	G	B	A	W	T	A	S	R	M	T	A	B
A	R	E	L	O	H	C	P	A	Y	I	Y	R	R	P
V	A	C	C	I	N	A	T	I	O	N	B	F	S	L
A	N	T	I	B	I	O	T	I	C	S	G	L	W	A
M	Z	X	Z	Y	W	Y	A	D	Z	I	Z	O	E	A

2 Reorder the words to find the definitions or descriptions of the key terms in bold. The terms are all related to diseases and immunity. The first one has been done for you.

Pathogens: that are diseases organisms cause

Pathogens are organisms that cause diseases.

a **Transmissible diseases**: that transferred can be from person one

   Diseases that ....

   .... to another.

b **Active immunity**: the of response immunity is of the body direct

   This type ....

   to a pathogen.

c **Passive immunity**: antibodies ready-made of requires from another immunity

   This type ....

   .... source.

LANGUAGE TIP

Type of, variety of and *kind of* are useful phrases to use when giving definitions of categories of things:

Paracetamol is a *type of* analgesic or painkiller.

d **Antibodies**: complementary to a antigens shape

These have ....

e **Antigens**: These the outside found are pathogens usually on of

....

f **Antibiotics**: taken medication down bacteria to slow the of growth

....

Exercise 10.2 Cholera

IN THIS EXERCISE YOU WILL:

Science skills:

- understand how the body is affected by cholera.

English skills:

- answer questions relating to *affect* and *effect*.

Cholera is a disease that affects the human gut. This exercise is aimed at helping you to identify what cholera is and how cholera can affect the gut.

Read the passage and answer the questions.

Cholera is an infection caused by a bacterium called *Vibrio cholerae*, which is found in dirty water or contaminated food. Many common symptoms affect the human body when the bacteria are found in the human gut. These symptoms include:

- diarrhoea
- nausea
- dehydration
- vomiting
- painful stomach cramps

It is estimated by the World Health Organization that there are millions of cases of cholera every year. Failure to treat cholera can lead to death, and thousands of people die each year. Cholera can be prevented by providing safe, clean water and proper sanitation.

3 **a** State the name of the bacterium that causes cholera.

....

b State the name of the part of the body that the bacterium affects.

....

c State the effects that cholera can have on the answer to part **b**.

....

LANGUAGE TIP

Several key terms related to disease and immunity begin with the letter 'A'. Here is a tip to help you differentiate between two of them:

1 *Antigen* helps with *antibody generating*.

2 *Antibodies* are produced in response to things that are *anti-* our *bodies*.

LANGUAGE TIP

State is a useful command word. It means 'say' or 'give' (information, a name etc.).

d Write two sentences that suggest how cholera can be prevented.

....

4 Read the sentences and choose the correct option.

   a One of the possible **affects** / **effects** of cholera is vomiting.

   b Cholera can also **affect** / **effect** the water levels in your blood.

   c Only drinking clean water can **affect** / **effect** your chances of contracting cholera.

   d Painful stomach cramps is a negative **affect** / **effect** of having cholera.

   e Feeling better and being healthier also have a positive **affect** / **effect** on your mental health.

> **LANGUAGE TIP**
>
> See Exercise 5.2 for information on using *affect* and *effect*.

Exercise 10.3 Immunity army

> **IN THIS EXERCISE YOU WILL:**
>
> Science skills:
>
> • describe how the body protects itself from disease and infection.
>
> English skills:
>
> • use comparisons to understand a biological concept.

In order to demonstrate your understanding of immunity, you should be able to describe how the body protects itself from pathogens, infection and disease.

> **LANGUAGE FOCUS**
>
> To show how alike two or more things are, we use comparisons:
>
> To describe things as alike, use *like* and *similar to*. (We call this kind of sentence an analogy.)
>
> To say they are not alike, use *different from* or *different to*.
>
> After *like, similar to, different to* and *different from* you need a noun phrase. You can continue the sentence with *that* + verb or with *-ing*:
>
> The human body is *like* the land being defended.
>
> Pathogens are *similar to* an army invading the country.
>
> The antibodies are *different from* the pathogens invading the body.

5 Complete the following comparisons:

   a The human .... is like the territory being defended. The cells are like the people that live in the territory.

   b The .... are the enemy that want to invade the territory.

c The body's first line of .... is similar to walls, mountains and the sea that keep the bad guys out.

d The second line of defence is like a regular army of .... patrolling the territory. The third line of defence is similar to special forces that are able to target certain bad guys.

6 Answer the questions to check your understanding.

a Which type of white blood cell is most similar to regular soldiers patrolling the territory?

....

b Explain your answer to part **a**.

....

....

c The special forces identify a possible enemy. Write your own analogy for how the special forces soldiers will be able to identify a potential enemy.

....

....

d Write your own set of analogies for how the body protects itself against disease. If you are struggling, you may be able to find plenty of inspiration on the internet. Think about defending a building, or a sports goal / area.

....

....

....

....

....

7 Write sentences of your own using the words given. Think of examples from your own life or experience to help you remember the meaning of each word.

Antibiotics ....

....

Antibodies ....

....

Symptoms ....

....

Effects ....

....

> Chapter 11

Respiration and gas exchange

IN THIS CHAPTER YOU WILL:

Science skills:

- outline how respiration releases energy from glucose

- describe the role of gas exchange and ventilation in humans.

English skills:

- use nouns, adjectives and verbs to describe what happens to energy released as a result of respiration

- use *while* and *whereas* to express contrast between aerobic and anaerobic respiration

- use the plural form and singular form for key words related to the lungs.

Exercise 11.1 Equations of respiration

IN THIS EXERCISE YOU WILL:

Science skills:

- write the word equation for aerobic respiration and understand the position of reactants and products in chemical equations.

English skills:

- use key scientific terms to explain or define a word equation.

KEY WORDS

aerobic respiration: chemical reactions that take place in mitochondria, which use oxygen to break down glucose and other nutrient molecules to release energy for the cell to use

product: the new substance formed by a chemical reaction

To begin to understand respiration, you need to know what is required for respiration and what the products are. This can be represented by word equations and chemical equations to show exactly what happens in the **aerobic respiration** reaction.

1   Solve the anagrams to find key terms related to chemical equations and use the terms to complete the passage that follows.

   a   tanrtcea   ....

   b   creatsnat   ....

   c   iortneacs   ....

   d   durpoct   ....

   e   rodcsutp   ....

   f   quioetan   ....

Chemical .... are shown by an .... The .... are

written before the arrow. The .... are written after the arrow.

For example: *glucose + oxygen* → *carbon dioxide + water*

A .... is something that reacts, so it is always the first part of the

equation. A .... is something that is made as a consequence of the

reaction and is written at the end of the equation.

                      glucose → lactic acid

                     reactant   product

2   Read the text, then answer the questions below.

> Respiration is a chemical reaction that releases energy from nutrients such as glucose. Oxygen is required for the reaction to take place, and the products released are carbon dioxide and water. These are 'waste' products and are removed from the cell after respiration.

   a   For respiration to take place, two reactants are required. Write the names of the reactants below.

       ....

   b   The chemical reaction of respiration produces two waste **products**. Write the names of the products below.

       ....

   c   Respiration has a third important product that is very useful for the growth and repair of our bodies. What is the useful product of respiration?

       ....

   d   The respiration reaction can be summarised as an equation. Enter the answers to the questions above into the equation for respiration below.

       .... + ... → .... + ...

LANGUAGE TIP

In science, the verb *require* is used more frequently than *need*, so:

oxygen is required = oxygen is needed.

Exercise 11.2 The importance of respiration

IN THIS EXERCISE YOU WILL:

Science skills:

- explain why energy from respiration is important.

English skills:

- use nouns, adjectives and verbs to describe what happens to energy released as a result of respiration.

LANGUAGE FOCUS

Many words are part of 'word families' – they have the same root. The group of letters at the end of the word, or suffix, will often tell you the word's form, for example *-tion* or *-sion* words are nouns:

expand (verb) → expan*sion* (noun)

Your chest expands when you breathe in.

The expansion of your chest makes room for air.

With some verbs, the past participle can be used as an adjective. This kind of adjective usually describes a reaction or the consequence of an action. For example:

I am interested in biology. (*interested* = my reaction to biology)

Expanded lungs contain more air than contracted lungs (*expanded, contracted* = the consequences of actions)

3 Complete the table with the correct form. The words are all related to how animals and plants use energy.

Verb	Noun	Past participle as adjective
contract	contraction	contracted
link	linking	....
divide	....	divided
concentrate	concentration	....
....	transmission	transmitted
....	....	produced

LANGUAGE TIP

You can only use *transmitted* and *produced* as part of two-word adjectives, such as *a physically-transmitted disease*, *a mass-produced car*.

4   Use the correct word form from the table in question **3** to complete each sentence. Each sentence describes a process that requires energy.

    a   Internal body temperature must be kept constant, so heat is .... when the external environment is cold.

    b   Damaged tissues grow and repair by the process of cell ....

    c   Movement of the body is allowed by muscle ....

    d   The movement of molecules against the .... gradient is required for active transport to take place.

    e   Amino acids are .... together to form protein molecules.

    f   Messages are sent around the body by the .... of nerve impulses to and from the different parts of the body.

Exercise 11.3 Aerobic and anaerobic respiration

IN THIS EXERCISE YOU WILL:

Science skills:

*   write the word equations for aerobic and anaerobic respiration.

English skills:

*   use *while* and *whereas* to express contrast.

KEY WORDS

anaerobic respiration: chemical reactions in cells that break down nutrient molecules to release energy, without using oxygen

So far, you have looked at aerobic respiration. This means that the reaction involves oxygen.

Sometimes, there is no oxygen available. An organism may still be able to respire, and produce a small amount of energy, without *oxygen*. This is called **anaerobic respiration**.

You can improve your understanding of the two types of respiration by using the different equations related to them:

aerobic: glucose + oxygen → carbon dioxide + water

anaerobic: glucose → lactic acid

Anaerobic respiration in humans is the breakdown of glucose into energy and produces lactic acid. These products are different from the products of aerobic respiration that you covered in Exercise 11.1.

LANGUAGE FOCUS

In Chapter 2 we looked at describing differences and contrast. Here we will look at two more words you can use to express contrast: *while* and *whereas*.

When expressing contrast, *while* and *whereas* have the same meaning and that meaning is similar to *but*.

You can use *while* and *whereas* to start a sentence, or in the middle after a comma. Remember: *but* can only be used in the middle of a sentence.

Whereas aerobic respiration requires oxygen, anaerobic respiration does not.

Aerobic respiration requires oxygen, *whereas* anaerobic respiration does not.

While aerobic respiration releases lots of energy, anaerobic respiration releases a small amount of energy.

Anaerobic respiration releases a small amount of energy, *while* aerobic respiration releases a lot.

---

5 Complete the table with a sentence about the differences and similarities between aerobic and anaerobic respiration in humans. In your sentences about differences, refer to both aerobic and anaerobic respiration using *whereas* or *while*. Use the list of words below to help. The first one has been done for you.

glucose   small amounts of energy   requires oxygen   reactant

release(s) energy   break down food   produces lactic acid

large amounts of energy   does not require oxygen

Similarities	Differences
Both use glucose as a reactant.	Aerobic respiration produces carbon dioxide and water, whereas anaerobic respiration produces lactic acid.

Exercise 11.4 Gas exchange in humans

IN THIS EXERCISE YOU WILL:

Science skills:

* describe what happens during gas exchange in human lungs.

English skills:

* use the plural form and singular form for key words related to the lungs.

Oxygen is taken into the body through the mouth and it is transferred to the blood at the lungs. There are several parts of the body that the oxygen molecules will pass through on their journey (Figure 11.1).

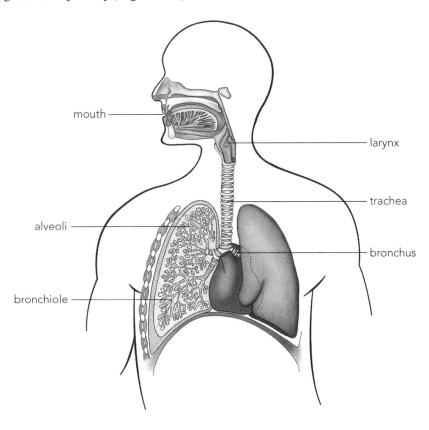

Figure 11.1: The breathing system.

6 Use the words given to write a sentence about the breathing system. Here is an example to help you:

breathe, mouth, oxygen

We breathe in oxygen through our mouth.

a oxygen, passed, towards, lungs, trachea

....

....

b bronchus, divides, bronchiole, lungs

....

....

c gas, exchange, alveoli

....

....

LANGUAGE FOCUS

The origins of English words are very varied and come from several languages. Many words in biology and other sciences come from Latin or Greek.
This means that, although most nouns in the plural form in English end in -s, some words have a different plural form.

Words that end with -us in the singular often end with -i in the plural: bronchus – bronchi, alveolus – alveoli

Words that end with -a in the singular often end with -ae in the plural: formula – formulae, antenna – antennae

Words that end with -um in the singular often end with -a in the plural: bacterium – bacteria

7 Write these words in the correct column of the table. The first pair has been done for you.

alveoli   bronchiole   lung   bronchi   bronchus   lungs

bronchioles   alveolus

Singular term	Plural term
lung	lungs

Exercise 11.5 Breathing in and breathing out

IN THIS EXERCISE YOU WILL:

Science skills:

- describe what happens during human ventilation.

English skills:

- write about breathing using the correct terms.

Humans need oxygen for respiration and they need to remove waste products such as carbon dioxide. This happens by inhalation (breathing in) and exhalation (breathing out).

Look at Figure 11.2, then answer the questions that follow.

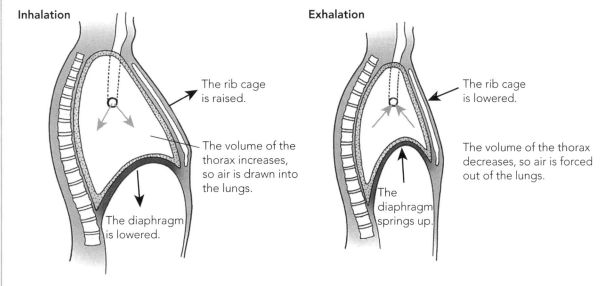

Inhalation

The rib cage is raised.

The volume of the thorax increases, so air is drawn into the lungs.

The diaphragm is lowered.

Exhalation

The rib cage is lowered.

The volume of the thorax decreases, so air is forced out of the lungs.

The diaphragm springs up.

Figure 11.2: Inhalation and exhalation.

LANGUAGE TIP

Prefixes can help make words easy to remember:

In- is the prefix for *in*halation; this is where we breathe *in*.

Ex- is the prefix for *ex*halation; this is where carbon dioxide *exits* through breathing out.

Re- is the prefix for *re*spiration; this where we breathe again and again *repeatedly*.

8 Read the paragraph and circle the correct word from the options available to describe the stages of breathing in.

The muscles of the diaphragm **contract / relax**, which pulls the diaphragm **upwards / downwards**. The external intercostal muscles **contract / relax** and pull the rib cage **downwards / upwards**. This **increases / decreases** the volume of the thorax and air rushes **into / out of** the lungs. The air rushes in because the pressure in the lungs is lower than that outside the body.

9 Complete the table to show what happens to the body during exhalation. The first one has been completed for you.

Part of the breathing system	What happens to this part
diaphragm	relaxes
external intercostal muscles	....
rib cage	....
thorax volume	....
pressure in the lungs compared to outside the body	....

10 Write a paragraph to describe what happens during exhalation (breathing out). Use the information from the table in question **9**. The paragraph should be similar in structure to the paragraph in question **8**.

....

....

....

....

....

....

....

....

....

....

Chapter 12

Coordination and response

Science skills:

- outline how humans respond to stimuli
- describe how hormones produce a response.

English skills:

- use adverbs to describe differences between the nervous system and the endocrine system.

Exercise 12.1 Responding to stimuli

IN THIS EXERCISE YOU WILL:

Science skills:

- use key words related to coordination and response.

English skills:

- read a passage and identify key words.

KEY WORD

stimulus (plural: stimuli): a change in the environment that can be detected by organisms

This exercise will remind you what your basic senses are. It will also give you practice in reading a text and recognising key words. You should always identify the key words when you read a text in a book, or a question in an assessment.

LANGUAGE FOCUS

Key words are important in any area – science, art, sport, etc. – as they help you identify the general topic of a text or conversation, and focus your own writing.

For example:

You see / hear	You know the text is about
cell, membrane, leaf, chlorophyll	plants
gut, stomach, liver	digestion
lungs, anaerobic	respiration
arteries, veins, capillaries	circulatory system

When you read a text, remember to circle, underline or highlight the key words, check the meaning, if necessary, and use these key words to build and focus your answers.

Remember also to check you know the correct spelling, the plural form, if the term is a noun, verb, adjective, etc. so you can use it in a sentence, and that you know other forms, where relevant. For example:

leaf – leaves, stimulus – stimuli

digest, digestion, digestive (system)

anaerobic spelling = *an + aero + bic*

There are five senses. Each sense is carried out by a certain sense organ.

1   Find the names of the five sense organs in the word string. Write them on the line below.

noseeareyetongueskin

....

2   Use the words from question **1** to label the sense organs in this diagram.

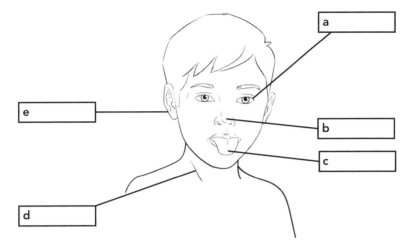

3   Use the diagram in question **2** to help you complete the table with the correct sense organs. You should match each organ with the **stimuli** given.

Sense organ	Stimuli detected
a	vision, light
b	hearing, balance
c	smell, chemical
d	taste, chemical
e	touch, pain, temperature

4   a   Read about Marcus's morning, and underline **eight** actions or states in the text that talk about sensory experiences.

> Marcus wakes up when he hears his alarm clock ring at 6.15 a.m. He touches the snooze button on his alarm clock and closes his eyes again. Suddenly, he hears someone outside his room, and the door opens. Marcus can smell something delicious as his mother switches the light on. He rubs his sleepy eyes. Mmmm! He can see his mother with a plate of pancakes and a glass of fruit juice – they smell amazing. Marcus eats his breakfast quickly. He can taste blueberries and syrup in the pancakes – wonderful! Marcus smiles at his mother and gets up, ready for a day of learning at school.

b Now match the actions or states you have underlined to the correct sensory organ.

For example: He hears his alarm clock – ears.

....

....

....

....

Exercise 12.2 Reflex arcs

IN THIS EXERCISE YOU WILL:

Science skills:

- explain why reflex arcs are important for survival.

English skills:

- use the verb *carry* correctly in sentences.

KEY WORDS

neurone: a cell that is specialised for conducting electrical impulses rapidly

reflex action: a means of automatically and rapidly integrating and coordinating stimuli with the responses of effectors

reflex arc: a series of neurones (sensory, relay and motor) that transmit electrical impulses from a receptor to an effector

A **reflex action** is an automatic response to a stimulus, for example pulling your hand away if you accidentally put it on something hot. In a reflex action, signals pass through three types of **neurone** in a **reflex arc**.

Table 12.1 introduces the three types of neurone that are involved in reflexes.

Type of neurone	Role in a reflex arc
sensory	carries electrical impulse from the receptors to the central nervous system
motor	carries electrical impulses from the central nervous system to the effectors (muscles or glands)
relay	connects a sensory neurone to a motor neurone

Table 12.1: The role of different neurones in reflex actions.

LANGUAGE TIP

The verb *carry* is frequently used in biology. Its meaning is similar to *hold, take, transport from one place (or time) to another*. So:

Neurones *carry* electric impulses.

And:

DNA *carries* genetic information.

Can you think of other examples?

5 Use the information in Table 12.1 to complete this diagram.

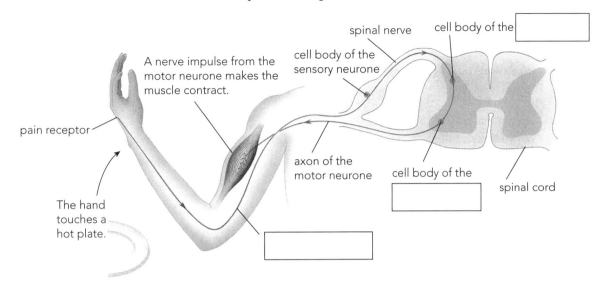

You do not need to know any details of the terms axon and cell body, as they are beyond the requirements of the syllabus.

6 Find and cross out the error in each of the sentences below. Then write the correct sentence in the space below. Use the information in question **5** to help you.

Here is an example to help you:

A ~~reflex~~ detects a stimulus and converts it into an electrical impulse.

A receptor detects a stimulus and converts it into an
electrical impulse.

a The electrical reaction is carried to the central nervous system by a sensory neurone.

....

....

b The electrical impulse is supported by a relay neurone across the spinal cord.

....

....

c The electrical impulse is then carried away from the central nervous system along a relay neurone.

....

....

d The motor neurone throws the electrical impulse to an effector.

....

e An organ is a muscle or gland that carries out the response to the stimulus.

....

....

f A reflex action is a voluntary response to a stimulus.

....

g The plural of stimulus is stimuluses.

....

7 Read this text about two reflex actions, then complete the table by adding the missing words and information.

> A doctor may tap your knee to locate the tendon that lies beneath the kneecap. This tapping stretches the tendon, which produces the 'knee jerk' reflex action. This reflex action occurs because the muscles in the upper thigh contract to cause the leg to straighten. Without this reflex action, the body would not be able to support its own weight during walking.
>
> When you eat some food, you rely on the automatic response of swallowing to ingest the food. When your throat makes contact with the food particles, it causes a muscle above the trachea to contract. This means that food cannot enter the trachea and it prevents damage to the lungs.

Reflex action	Stimulus	Response	Survival value
knee jerk	tendon stretched by tapping kneecap	upper .... muscles contract	.... supports body weight when walking
swallowing			

Exercise 12.3 Nervous system versus endocrine system

IN THIS EXERCISE YOU WILL:

Science skills:

*   compare the nervous system and the endocrine system.

English skills:

*   use adverbs to describe differences between different systems.

KEY WORD

adrenaline: a hormone secreted by the adrenal glands, which prepares the body for fight or flight

This exercise will help you to understand the differences between the endocrine system and the nervous system.

8   The endocrine system has similarities and differences with the nervous system. Read the following passage and select the correct words to describe the endocrine system.

The endocrine system consists of **glands / tissue** that release electrical **impulses / hormones**. Some of the glands produce hormones with similar names, which makes them easier to remember. An example of this is the thyroid gland, which produces the **thyroxine / adrenaline** hormone. This hormone controls the metabolism of the body. The **adrenal / pituitary** gland produces a hormone called **adrenaline**. Adrenaline is secreted into the blood and may make your **heart / lungs** beat faster when you are excited or scared. The testes are found in **males / females** and produce the **testosterone / progesterone** hormone. This hormone is important in reaching puberty and affects levels of growth of **facial hair / hips** in men.

9   The table below contains information about the endocrine system and the nervous system. Use your knowledge of these systems and the key words listed here to complete the table. Two of the answers have been completed for you.

electrical impulses   hormones   longer amount of time

neurones   nerve fibres   quickly   secretory cells   slowly

Feature	Nervous system	Endocrine system
consists of		
information transmitted by		
message sent along		blood vessels
speed at which impulse travels		
length of time the effect lasts for	short amount of time	

LANGUAGE FOCUS

Adverbs of manner (descriptive adverbs) are used to give us extra information about a verb. Most adverbs are formed by adding *-ly* to the adjective form of a word, and can be used to describe what is happening in a biological process. For example:

Does an electrical impulse travel *quickly* or *slowly*?

The electrical impulses travel very *quickly*.

What is a volatile reaction? It is when chemicals react *violently*.

Other adverbs include *suddenly, increasingly, easily, carefully, scientifically*.

Note that:

- adjectives that end with *-y*: change the *y* to *i*, so *easy* → *easily*.

- adjectives that end with *-l*: double the *-l*, so *careful* → *carefully*.

- adjectives that end with *-ic*: add *ally*, so *scientific* → *scientifically*.

- adverbs that do not end in *-ly* include *fast* and *hard* (She works *hard*.).

10 Complete the sentences with the correct adverb form of the adjectives given.

    a   When your hand touches a hot pan, your muscles contract (quick) ....

    b   If your eyes are dry, you blink (involuntary) ....

    c   The nervous system affects areas of the body (selective) ....

    d   Electrical impulses travel through the nervous system very (fast) ....

11 Circle the correct adverb to complete the sentences.

    a   When adrenaline is produced, the breathing rate increases **gradually / rapidly**.

    b   If the motor neurone is working **efficiently / inefficiently**, it will cause the muscle to contract.

    c   If you are scared or excited, you might breathe **with more difficulty / more easily**.

    d   It's a good idea to eat something sweet before an exam, because stress causes the body to burn sugar more **rapidly / slowly**.

12 Now compare the two systems by completing these sentences using adverbs of manner.

    a   In the nervous system, the ....

        but in the ....

        ....

    b   The nervous system is made up of ....

        while the ....

        ....

    c   In the endocrine system, information is ....

        whereas ....

        ....

    d   In the nervous system, the message is sent along ....

        while in the ....

        ....

    e   In the endocrine system, the effect lasts for ....

        but in the ....

        ....

Chapter 13

Excretion and homeostasis

IN THIS CHAPTER YOU WILL:

Science skills:

- identify key words associated with excretion and homeostasis

- describe how waste products are removed from the body.

English skills:

- use *which* and *this* to connect statements about homeostasis to their explanations

- convert passive sentences into active sentences to describe stages in the human excretory system.

Exercise 13.1 Key concepts in excretion and homeostasis

IN THIS EXERCISE YOU WILL:

Science skills:

- identify the key concepts for excretion and homeostasis.

English skills:

- compare similar key words to each other.

KEY WORDS

excretion: the removal of the waste products of metabolism and substances in excess of requirements

glucagon: a hormone secreted by the pancreas, which increases blood glucose concentration

homeostasis: the maintenance of a constant internal environment

ureter: one of a pair of tubes that carries urine from the kidneys to the bladder

urethra: the tube that carries urine from the bladder to the outside

vasoconstriction: narrowing of arterioles, caused by the contraction of the muscle in their walls

vasodilation: widening of arterioles, caused by the relaxation of the muscle in their walls

1   Find and separate 13 key words related to **excretion** and **homeostasis** in the word-snake below.

excretionkidneysistureterurethranephrondeaminationfiltrationreabsorption
homeostasisinsulinglucagonhypothalamusvasodilation

Some key words in this topic are similar to each other. Using the correct key word at the appropriate time is important when trying to show your understanding.

LANGUAGE FOCUS

We have already seen various ways of expressing difference, for example in Chapter 2. Here is another way:

Person A has *more* concentrated urine *than* person B.

This process requires *less* energy *than* others.

More … than and *less … than* are often used with adjectives to form comparative adjectives, but they are also used with nouns (*urine*, *energy*) to imply a difference in quantity of something.

Also remember that after a statement or description, you can use *but* and an auxiliary verb to express contrast. The auxiliary (*does, did, has,* etc.) will be in the same tense as the verb in the first part of the sentence, but one will be positive and one will be negative.

         +   –
The kidney has nephrons, but the liver does not.

         –   +
Subject A *did not have* upstanding hairs, *but* subject B *did.*

Emphasising similarity:

The two glands *both* release hormones.

Both glands release hormones.

Use *both* in front of the verb or the noun when it is important to stress the fact that two things carry out the same action. (NOTE: use *both* after *are* and *were*.)

2   Complete the sentences using the word in brackets and your own ideas.
    For example:
    In summer, people excrete more sweat (than) than they do in the winter

    a   The liver does not have nephrons (but) ....

    b   Some toxins are excreted in the urine (but) ....

    c   The liver and lungs are (both) ....

    d   When doing sport, you should drink (than) ....

3 For the following pairs of words, write a sentence to make a comparison that will help you to remember the function / role of each word. Use the example sentences in the Language Focus box to help you.

ureter, **urethra**

....

....

glucose, **glucagon**

....

....

vasodilation, **vasoconstriction**

....

....

LANGUAGE TIP

Remember, when the glucose is gone, glucagon comes along.

Exercise 13.2 Homeostasis

IN THIS EXERCISE YOU WILL:

Science skills:

- describe how homeostasis maintains a constant internal environment.

English skills:

- use *which* and *this* to help write explanations and definitions.

KEY WORD

metabolism: the chemical reactions that take place in living organisms

This exercise will help you construct sentences that contain the correct word to describe what is happening in our bodies during homeostasis.

Homeostasis is the maintenance of a constant environment inside the body. This is crucial for organisms to continue to survive, grow healthily and work efficiently. Maintaining constant temperature, water levels and sugar levels ensures that our bodies can adjust to whatever the external conditions of the body may be.

4 Circle the correct words to describe what happens when body temperature is falling.

When the external environment is cold, the body responds by doing the following:

a Shivering begins – **rapid** / **slow** contraction of muscles.

b Metabolism **decreases** / **increases** – releases more heat energy.

c Hair becomes **flat** / **erect** – traps an insulating layer of air at the skin surface.

d Capillaries near to the surface of the skin become **wider** / **narrower** – reduces the amount of heat lost.

e Sweat glands produce **less** / **more** sweat – to prevent evaporation.

LANGUAGE FOCUS

To write explanations, we can connect a statement and an explanation using the word *which*. This helps to avoid repetition, For example:

When humans are cold, shivering begins. Shivering is a rapid contraction of muscles.

When humans are cold, shivering begins, which is a rapid contraction of muscles.

The first part of the sentence ends with a comma (,) before *which*.

5 Sentences a–e in question **4** are written in note form. Add *which* to form complete sentences and explanations. The first one has been done for you.

a Shivering begins, which is the rapid contraction of muscles.

b **Metabolism** ....

c Hair becomes ....

d Capillaries ....

e Sweat glands ....

LANGUAGE TIP

In a longer sentence, to avoid repetition, you can also start a new sentence with *This*.

When humans are cold, shivering begins. *This* is a rapid contraction of muscles.

---

6   Write the sentences again, this time using two sentences and *This*, as shown in the Language Tip above.

a   Shivering ....

b   Metabolism ....

c   Hair becomes ....

d   Capillaries ....

e   Sweat glands ....

Exercise 13.3 The human excretory system

IN THIS EXERCISE YOU WILL:

Science skills:

• describe how waste products are removed from the body.

English skills:

• convert passive sentences into active sentences.

KEY WORD

urea: a waste product produced in the liver, from the breakdown of excess amino acids

---

The many reactions that occur in our cells produce waste products that must be removed from the body. The excretory system ensures that this happens.

7   On Figure 13.1, four parts of the excretory system are indicated.

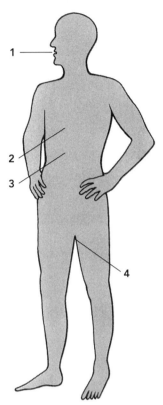

Figure 13.1: Parts of the excretory system.

The four statements in the table below can be connected to the numbers in the diagram. They are also connected to the following organs.

kidneys   liver   lungs

Complete the table with the number that indicates where each excretory process takes place and the name of the excretory organ(s) involved in each process. You will use one organ name twice.

Statement	Number on diagram	Name of organ(s)
Carbon dioxide produced during respiration is excreted here.	....	....
Bile pigments produced here are excreted in faeces.	....	....
Urea (proteins that have been broken into smaller pieces) excreted by this organ is passed out in the urine.	....	....
Excess water and salts are removed by this organ.	....	....

LANGUAGE FOCUS

In Chapters 4 and 7 you saw how to turn active sentences into passive sentences. To turn a passive sentence into an active one you follow the reverse process. Look:

The carbon dioxide produced during respiration *is excreted by the lungs.* = passive

The lungs excrete the carbon dioxide produced during respiration. = active

1   Look for the word(s) after *by* in the passive sentence. This will start your active sentence:

The lungs …

2   Look at the tense of *be* in the passive sentence. This tells you the tense of your active verb:

The lungs (present tense) …

3   Look at the participle after *be* in the passive sentence. This gives you the verb for the active sentence. Write it in the tense from Step 2:

The lungs excrete …

4   Look at the words before *be* in the passive sentence. These come after your verb in the active sentence.

The lungs excrete carbon dioxide produced during respiration.

Choose between active and passive depending on what you want to emphasise – the thing doing the action (the lungs – active) or the thing that receives the action (the carbon dioxide – passive).

8   Using the information from the table in question **7**, turn the passive sentences below into active sentences. You will need to use the words *kidneys* and *liver* in your answers.

a   Bile pigments produced here are excreted in faeces.

The liver produces .... which ....

....

b   **Urea** excreted by this organ is passed out in the urine.

.... which ....

....

c   Excess water and salts are removed.

....

Chapter 14

Reproduction in plants

IN THIS CHAPTER YOU WILL:

Science skills:

- understand the key terms associated with asexual and sexual reproduction
- link different parts of a flower to their function.

English skills:

- use linkers of sequence and of result to outline sexual reproduction in plants
- show the differences between types of pollination using comparative sentences.

Exercise 14.1 Asexual and sexual reproduction

IN THIS EXERCISE YOU WILL:

Science skills:

- identify the key words associated with asexual and sexual reproduction.

English skills:

- identify key words in a text and convert to concise information that can be added to a table.

KEY WORDS

asexual reproduction: a process resulting in the production of genetically identical offspring from one parent

sexual reproduction: a process involving the fusion of two gametes to form a zygote and the production of offspring that are genetically different from each other

Sexual reproduction and **asexual reproduction** not only sound similar but also have many similar key words. Understanding the difference between them is essential for you to demonstrate your knowledge.

1 Find these words in the word search:

asexual   **gametes**   **genetically**   **offspring**

ovum   **reproduction**   **sperm**   **zygote**

R	S	I	I	W	A	P	V	W	Y	K	E	G	Y	O
Q	E	E	C	V	I	B	H	S	I	U	V	L	W	F
G	W	P	T	W	I	I	A	S	E	X	U	A	L	F
V	U	X	R	E	I	I	Q	B	D	E	S	G	I	S
D	Q	G	R	O	M	G	A	I	V	B	E	G	H	P
O	I	H	V	N	D	A	K	T	N	N	I	X	D	R
Z	Y	G	O	T	E	U	G	J	E	R	G	Y	S	I
K	D	C	Q	D	P	L	C	T	O	H	Z	N	R	N
F	L	T	B	L	W	Q	I	T	H	F	M	F	F	G
G	Z	T	S	B	M	C	K	M	I	L	C	X	V	N
M	O	T	Z	L	A	I	O	A	S	O	D	V	T	K
R	K	I	K	L	Q	M	Q	F	V	X	N	H	M	N
E	P	V	L	A	C	I	T	N	E	D	I	U	I	G
P	F	Y	W	C	L	R	H	G	T	A	V	X	I	O
S	D	L	S	K	N	P	R	J	Z	O	H	M	U	V

2 You have identified the key words associated with sexual reproduction and asexual reproduction. Add each of these key words to the table and write a short sentence about each one. The sentence should be written in the correct column for either sexual or asexual reproduction. Some words might apply to both columns. One has been done for you.

> **LANGUAGE TIP**
>
> Asexual reproduction requires only one parent. Asexual starts with 'a' which we could use to say, 'a single parent', or 'a single thing'. This can help you remember that asexual reproduction only requires one ('a') parent.

Key word	Sexual reproduction	Asexual reproduction
Reproduction	Producing offspring from two parents.	Producing offspring from one parent.

Exercise 14.2 Sexual reproduction in plants

IN THIS EXERCISE YOU WILL:

Science skills:

- link reproductive parts of a flower to their function.

English skills:

- use sequencers for adding ideas in a logical sequence.

KEY WORD

pollination: the transfer of pollen grains from the male part of a plant (anther of stamen) to the female part of a plant (stigma)

Flowering plants can reproduce asexually as well as sexually. This happens when pollen (containing the male gametes) is transferred from one plant to another.

The first question in this section will help you to link the reproductive parts of the flower to their function. The second question will assess your ability to describe the process of sexual reproduction in plants.

3   Use Figure 14.1 to deduce which part of the flower performs a specific function and use this to complete the table. The description of the function contains clues as to which part of the plant it is referring to.

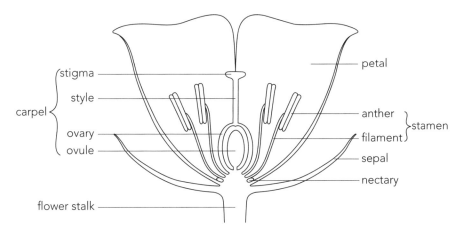

Figure 14.1: The structure of a flower.

Part of the plant	Function
	platform for pollen to land on
	the male part of the flower that is made up of the anther and the filament
	brightly coloured and scented to attract insects
	green part of the plant and protects the flower
	main stalk that holds the stigma in place
	hollow chamber from which the ovules develop
	female gamete found inside the ovary
	contains pollen grains and located at the end of the filament
	long stalk that holds the anther in place

LANGUAGE FOCUS

As well as using linkers for comparing and contrasting, we also use linkers to express sequence, and to express result. For example:

Sequencers: *First, then, next, after that, finally.*

Linkers of result: *as a result of this, this means, consequently.*

These linkers generally go at the start of the sentence.

Example of a sentence with a sequencer: *First*, the plant must absorb sunlight.

Example of a linker of result: *As a result of this*, the plant can photosynthesise.

Using linkers is like adding a signpost: it makes your paragraph much easier for the reader to follow and helps you to organise your thoughts logically and clearly.

4   Read the following statements about sexual reproduction in flowering plants, then rewrite them as full sentences using a linker of sequence or of result so that they form a paragraph. Choose from these linkers:

after this   as a result of this   finally   First

next   then   which means

For example:

Pollen that is released from an anther lands on the stigma – **pollination** occurs.

First, the pollen that is released from an anther lands on the stigma. Then pollination occurs.

The male and female gametes are haploid (contain half of the number of chromosomes).

Pollen tube forms down the style.

Delivers male gamete to the female gamete in the ovule.

Pollen tube finds gap in micropyle at the bottom of the style.

Fertilisation happens – the male and female gametes fuse together.

Zygote develops into an embryo and then a seed.

> You do not need to know any details of the term micropyle as it is beyond the requirements of the syllabus.

....

....

....

....

....

....

....

....

....

....

....

....

....

....

....

....

....

....

....

Exercise 14.3 Types of pollination

IN THIS EXERCISE YOU WILL:

Science skills:

- compare different ways that plants are pollinated.

English skills:

- write comparative sentences to show the differences between types of pollination.

Wind-pollinated flowers have a different structure to insect-pollinated flowers. The structure is different because each type of flower is best adapted to catch the different types of pollen that is transferred. Wind-pollinated flowers need to have stigmas that are open and available to catch pollen being moved by the wind. Insect-pollinated flowers must attract insects to bring the pollen directly to their stigma.

5   Table 14.1 shows the difference between the structure of wind-pollinated flowers and insect-pollinated flowers.

Insect-pollinated flower	Wind-pollinated flower
large, colourful petals, often with guide-lines	small, petals, less likely to be colourful, or no petals at all
often strongly scented	no scent
often have nectaries at the base of petals	no nectaries
anthers inside flower, where insect has to brush past them to reach nectar	anthers hang outside the flower, where they catch the wind
stigma inside flower, where insect has to brush past it to reach nectar	stigmas large and feathery and dangle outside the flower, where pollen in the air may land on it
sticky or spiky pollen grains, which stick to insects	smooth, light pollen, which can be blown in the wind
quite large quantities of pollen made, because some will be eaten or will be delivered to the wrong kind of flower	very large quantities of pollen made, because most will be blown away and lost

Table 14.1: A comparison between insect-pollinated and wind-pollinated flowers.

For each of the key terms below, write a comparative sentence to show the difference between wind-pollinated flowers and insect-pollinated flowers.
Refer to Chapter 2 for guidance on how to construct comparative sentences.

a   petals

....

b   nectaries

....

c   anthers

....

d   scent

....

e   stigma

....

f   pollen grains

....

g   quantity of pollen made

....

6   For the key terms below, write them in an appropriate biological sentence.
For example, for the key term *asexual reproduction*, you could write:

A farmer grows tomato plants and these reproduce by asexual reproduction.

a   sexual reproduction

....

....

b   gametes

....

....

c   wind-pollinated flowers

....

....

d   stigma

....

....

LANGUAGE TIP
Pollination requires the transfer of pollen from anther to stigma. This is another example where the key words are in alphabetical order: anther → stigma.

Chapter 15

Reproduction in humans

IN THIS CHAPTER YOU WILL:

Science skills:

- outline the structure and function of human sex cells

- compare puberty in males and females.

English skills:

- use the correct verb forms to describe the processes of fertilisation and implantation.

Exercise 15.1 Human sex cells

IN THIS EXERCISE YOU WILL:

Science skills:

- outline the main features of the male and female sex cells.

English skills:

- use the suffix -ing to describe what is happening.

LANGUAGE TIP

In scientific or formal writing, you can use *when + -ing* when you want to describe something as it happens, in the present tense. Look:

This supports the sperm cell *when it is swimming* towards the ovum (egg cell) → This supports the sperm cell, *when swimming* towards the ovum (egg cell).

KEY WORDS

chromosome: a length of DNA, found in the nucleus of a cell; it contains genetic information in the form of many different genes

mitochondria: small structures in a cell, where aerobic respiration releases energy from glucose

This exercise looks at the differences between human sex cells and compares the signs of sexual maturity in males and females. There are lots of key words and technical terms to put together into sentences.

1 Look at Figure 15.1 and complete the table to show how each part of the cell helps that cell to perform its job. The first one has been completed for you.

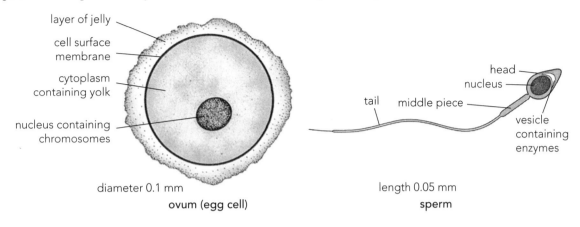

diameter 0.1 mm
ovum (egg cell)

length 0.05 mm
sperm

Figure 15.1: A sperm cell and an egg cell.

Feature of sex cell	Sperm or ovum (egg cell)	Function in sex cell
nucleus	both	contains the genetic information in the **chromosomes**
		supports the sperm cell when swimming towards the ovum (egg cell)
		is streamlined to reduce resistance when travelling
		prevents too many sperm from penetrating the egg at one time
		contains many **mitochondria** for powering the tail

2 a In the table in question **1** there are four words that end in *-ing*. Identify the four words and write them below.

....

....

....

....

b For each word, write a sentence that includes the word in a different context.

....

....

....

....

3 Read the following text and insert the appropriate key word into the table to match the correct description. The scientific key words in the text have been *italicised*.

The *sperm* must swim to the *ovum (egg cell)* and *fertilise* it within 24 hours of the egg being released from the *ovaries*. The ovum (egg cell) is released during *ovulation*, and travels along a tube called the *oviduct* where a sperm may fertilise it. The ovum (egg cell) is moved along the oviduct by *ciliated cells* and *peristalsis*.

Key word	Meaning
	female sex cell
	male sex cell
	fusing a sperm and an ovum (egg cell)
	tube that travels from the ovaries to the uterus
	the place where the ovum (egg cell) matures before release
	cells that contain small hairs to sweep the ovum (egg cell) along
	the monthly release of an ovum (egg cell) into the oviduct
	the contraction and relaxation of muscles to move the ovum (egg cell) along the oviduct

4 Three of the key words are parts of the female reproductive system. Write the names of these three parts below.

....

....

Exercise 15.2 Puberty in males and females

IN THIS EXERCISE YOU WILL:

Science skills:

• compare the changes in male and female bodies as a result of puberty.

English skills:

• use words to describe change.

KEY WORDS

hormones: chemicals that are produced by a gland and carried in the blood, which alter the activities of their specific target organs

puberty: the time at which sexual maturity is reached

Changes during **puberty** include some of the following: changes in behaviour, changes in the **hormones**, as well as physical changes to the body. The changes enable the person to be prepared to reproduce.

5   There are many words in this list that suggest a change is taking place, some of which you will see in the labels for the drawings below:

> **become   begin   broaden   develop   eventually**
>
> **gain   gradually   grow   quickly   start**

a   Write all of the words from the pictures that suggest a change as part of puberty in males and females.

Males: ....

Females: ....

b   There are five nouns related to puberty missing from the diagram – write the correct noun into the empty spaces marked **i** to **v**.

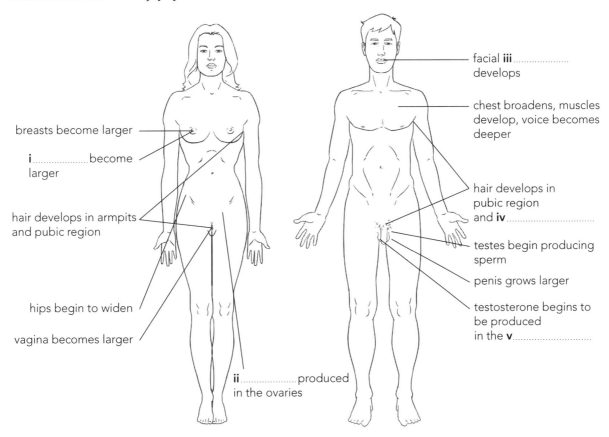

breasts become larger

i ....become larger

hair develops in armpits and pubic region

hips begin to widen

vagina becomes larger

ii ....produced in the ovaries

facial **iii** ....develops

chest broadens, muscles develop, voice becomes deeper

hair develops in pubic region and **iv** ....

testes begin producing sperm

penis grows larger

testosterone begins to be produced in the **v** ....

6   One type of change that happens in puberty is changes to the hormones (special chemicals) in our body. Complete the following sentences to describe these hormonal changes. Use the pictures in question **5** to help you.

   a   Women produce .... in the ....

   b   Men ....

7   Physical change refers to changes that happen to the body. Using the pictures in question **5** to help you, write the physical changes in the correct column in this table.

Women	Men

8   Hormonal changes are the reason other changes happen. We say that hormonal changes cause the other changes.

   Complete the sentences about how hormones cause other changes.

   a   Oestrogen production in women causes physical changes like ....

   ....

   b   Testosterone production ....

   ....

   ....

Exercise 15.3 Fertilisation and implantation

IN THIS EXERCISE YOU WILL:

Science skills:

- describe what happens during fertilisation and implantation.

English skills:

- use the correct verb forms to describe what is happening during fertilisation and implantation.

KEY WORDS

embryo: the ball of cells that is produced by repeated division of the zygote

implantation: attachment of the embryo to the lining of the uterus

zygote: a cell that is formed by the fusion of two gametes

LANGUAGE FOCUS

In Exercise 15.3, where you will complete sentences, it is important that your verb agreements are correct. Verb agreement is putting the correct verb form with its subject, like this: *I like, he/she/it likes, you like, we like, they like.*

Sometimes, however, the subject is a noun or noun phrase, not a pronoun (*I, you, it,* etc.). In this case, you must decide which verb form is correct by deciding if the noun is singular or plural. For example:

The/A zygote – This is one thing, so the verb is 'forms' (*it forms/joins* etc.).

gamete cells – This is plural, so the verb does not have an 's' (*they form/ join* etc.):

The/A zygote is a cell that *forms* when two gamete cells join.

Remember that in sentences, you can say The + singular, or (no The) plural. Be careful to use the correct verb form:

The zygote is a cell that *forms*… / Zygotes are cells that *form*…

The testis is often… / *Testes are* often…

Look at Figure 15.2 and use the verbs listed to complete the sentences in the text that follows.

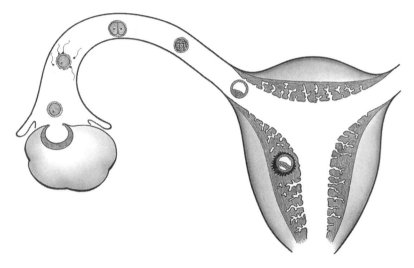

Figure 15.2: From ovulation to implantation.

9   Use these verbs in the correct form to complete the paragraph.

divide   form   form   fuse   move

reach   release   sink   support

First, ovaries .... a mature ovum (egg cell) into the oviduct. Then,

sperm .... the ovum (egg cell) and they .... to form a **zygote**.

We call this fertilisation. Next, the zygote .... This type of cell division

is mitosis. A ball of cells .... after many divisions. After that, the ball of

cells .... down the oviduct while dividing. We now call this an **embryo**.

Embryos .... into the soft lining of the uterus. We call this **implantation**.

At this stage, the placenta .... and .... the developing embryo.

> Chapter 16

Chromosomes, genes and proteins

IN THIS CHAPTER YOU WILL:

Science skills:

- describe the structure of a chromosome

- compare the processes of mitosis and meiosis

- use a Punnett square to calculate probability of offspring phenotypes.

English skills:

- recognise common prefixes and use modal verbs in sentences about inheritance

- use the correct verbs and expressions of probability when interpreting Punnet squares.

Exercise 16.1 Structure of a chromosome

IN THIS EXERCISE YOU WILL:

Science skills:

- identify the key words associated with the structure of a chromosome.

English skills:

- use prefixes to identify the meaning of a word.

KEY WORDS

alleles: alternative forms of a gene

gene: a length of DNA that codes for one protein

genotype: the genetic makeup of an organism in terms of the alleles present (e.g. GG)

phenotype: the observable features of an organism

This exercise will help you to understand the technical terms related to a chromosome and basic inheritance key words.

Note that the terms homologous, centromere and chromatids are used throughout this section. You do not need to know any details of these terms as they are beyond the requirements of the syllabus.

1   Separate the words in the word string below and write them in the spaces available. The first one has been completed for you.

chromatidchromosomeallelegenotypephenotypehomologouscentromerediploidhaploidgene

chromatid ....

....

....

....

....

2   Read the text and circle the correct option.

The two chromosomes from the mother and the father contain genetic information and are called homologous chromosomes. A chromosome is a **string / protein** of DNA that contains all of the **genetic / medical** information for that cell. A **gene** is a length of this DNA that we often refer to as the '**bundle / unit** of inheritance' and carries the code for specific proteins. Each gene has two different versions which can be expressed – these versions are called **alleles**. These alleles and your genes make up your **characteristics / nucleus** and when this information is shown as an observable characteristic it is known as the **phenotype**.

3   Now reread the text and answer the questions.

   a   Which word suggests that the genetic information will carry the code for one type of protein?

   ....

   b   Which adjective shows that there may be more than one type of the same gene?

   ....

   c   What is meant by the word *observable*?

   ....

   d   Give an example of an observable characteristic.

   ....

   e   What is the key word for the different versions of a particular gene?

   ....

LANGUAGE FOCUS

Key prefixes such as *homo, geno, pheno, centro* are clues as to the meaning of a key word.

Homo- means the same. For example, homologous means to have the same shape or location.

Geno- is related to family or birth. Your **genotype** is inherited from your parents.

Pheno- means to show. This is evident in phenotype which is a characteristic that we can see.

Centro- means related to the centre of something. The centromere is the central joining point of chromatids.

Understanding what these key prefixes mean can help you to understand the key words needed in this chapter.

4 Prefixes are commonly used in science and help you to understand the meaning of a word. Answer the following questions about common prefixes in inheritance as well as developing your understanding of key words.

a The prefix *chromo* means colour. Research the reason why scientists named the chromosome based on its colour.

....

....

b How does the prefix of the word *centromere* help you to remember where it is on a chromosome?

....

....

c *Pheno* means 'to show' and is a useful prefix in more ways than one. State the meaning of *phenotype*.

....

....

Exercise 16.2 Mitosis and meiosis

IN THIS EXERCISE YOU WILL:

Science skills:

- distinguish between the processes of mitosis and meiosis.

English skills:

- use modal verbs to describe what happens during cell division.

KEY WORDS

homozygous: having two identical alleles of a particular gene (e.g. GG or gg)

meiosis: division of a diploid nucleus resulting in four genetically different haploid nuclei; this is sometimes called a reduction division

mitosis: division of a cell nucleus resulting in two genetically identical nuclei (i.e. with the same number and kind of chromosomes as the parent nucleus)

Cell division relies on two key processes – **mitosis** and **meiosis**. You should be able to distinguish between these two types of cell division, and to look at diagrams of mitosis and meiosis and describe what is happening at the different stages.

Note that the terms homologous and chromatids are used throughout this section. You do not need to know any details of these terms as they are beyond the requirements of the syllabus.

LANGUAGE FOCUS

The 'modal verbs' are *can, could, may, might, will, would, shall, should* and *must*. One meaning of all modal verbs is related to certainty, possibility or probability.

The offspring *could* have blue eyes. (= it's possible)

The offspring *may* be **homozygous**. (= it's possible)

Their offspring *should* have black hair. (= it's almost certain, highly predictable)

All daughter cells *will* be genetically identical to the parent cell. (= it's certain)

The chromatids *would* be pulled apart by the spindle fibres. (= it's certain)

5   Look at Figure 16.1 showing the stages of mitosis and complete the sentences
    that follow.

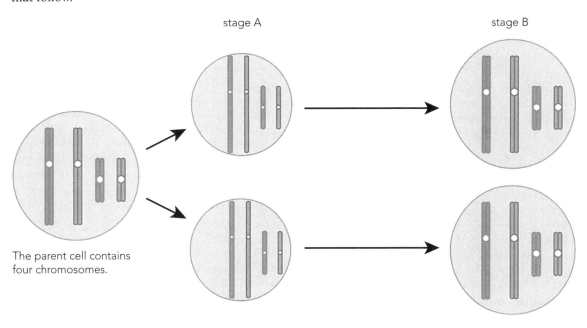

The parent cell contains
four chromosomes.

Figure 16.1: Stages of mitosis.

Select an appropriate modal verb from the list below to complete each sentence.
You can use the same modal verb more than once.

can   could   may   might   must

shall   should   will   would

a   The chromosomes .... be diploid at the beginning of the process.

b   During stage A, the chromosomes .... be separated.

c   The chromatids from each chromosome .... go into the daughter
    cell in stage A.

6 Figure 16.2 summarises what happens during meiosis. Use the diagram to answer the questions that follow.

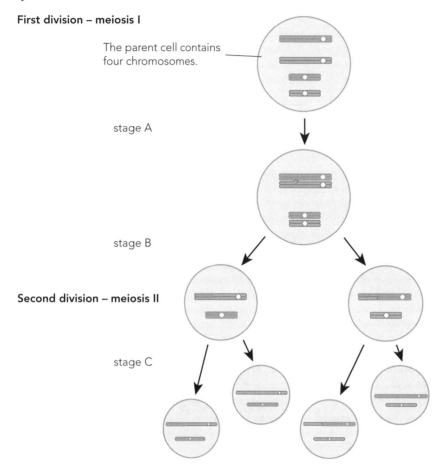

Figure 16.2: Stages of meiosis.

a Homologous chromosomes pair together during stage A. How many chromosomes make up a pair?

....

b How many daughter cells are present at stage B?

....

c What happens to the pair of homologous chromosomes during stage B?

....

d During stage C, the chromosomes separate into two chromatids. Where do these chromatids go to?

....

e How many daughter cells are produced at the end of one round of meiosis?

....

LANGUAGE TIP

Mitosis has two 'i's – use this to remember that the process produces *two* identical daughter cells. Meiosis contains an *e* and an *s* and produces eggs and sperm.

Exercise 16.3 Dominant and recessive alleles

IN THIS EXERCISE YOU WILL:

Science skills:

- distinguish between homozygous and heterozygous genotypes.

English skills:

- practise talking about alleles.

KEY WORDS

dominant allele: an allele that is expressed if it is present (e.g. G)

heterozygous: having two different alleles of a particular gene (e.g. Gg)

recessive allele: an allele that is only expressed when there is no dominant allele of the gene present (e.g. g)

Each cell in the body carries two different versions of a gene for any given characteristic. The two different versions are called alleles. You might carry genetic information for the brown phenotype eye colour but have an allele for blue eyes and an allele for brown eyes.

This task will give you practice at using the terms **dominant** and **recessive alleles** and lead into other key terms for this part of the chapter. You will need to read the information carefully in order to answer the questions that are in this exercise.

LANGUAGE FOCUS

Talking about alleles:

As well as *homo*, another important prefix in this chapter is *hetero*. As you saw in the previous exercises, *homo* refers to things that are the same.

Hetero- means 'different'. An example of this is heterotherms, which have a different body temperature depending on their situation.

In this exercise, **heterozygous** refers to when the two alleles for a particular gene are different. For example: Gg, Ff, Bb.

Also notice, we can use single letters as symbols for different alleles.

We use upper case (capital) letters for dominant alleles. For example, we can call the allele for brown eyes 'B'.

We use lower case (small) letters for recessive alleles. For example, we can call the allele for blue eyes 'b'.

Meet Heather and Casper.

Heather has blue eyes.
She has two alleles for
blue eyes.

Casper has brown eyes.
He has one allele for brown
eyes and one for blue eyes.

Figure 16.3: Characteristics of Heather and Casper.

Casper's allele for blue eyes has not had an effect on his observable characteristics. This is because he also has an allele for brown eyes.

7   Complete these sentences:

The allele for .... eyes is dominant over the allele for .... eyes.

The allele for .... eyes is recessive.

8   We say that Heather is homozygous and Casper is heterozygous.

   a   What does the prefix homo- mean? ....

   b   What does the prefix hetero- mean? ....

   c   What does it mean if someone is heterozygous? ....

   ....

9   Below are several pairs of alleles. State whether each one is homozygous or heterozygous. Here is an example to help you:

HH   ...*homozygous*...

   a   Hh   ....   **d**   XY   ....

   b   hh   ....   **e**   XX   ....

   c   Bb   ....   **f**   Ww   ....

10 Heather and Casper have a daughter. She has brown eyes.

a What allele has she received from Heather? ....

b How do you know this?

....

c What allele has she received from Casper? ....

d How do you know this?

....

....

Exercise 16.4 Codominance and blood groups

IN THIS EXERCISE YOU WILL:

Science skills:

- describe codominance in blood groups.

English skills:

- use the correct terms to denote how probable an outcome is.

KEY WORD

codominance: alleles that are both expressed in the phenotype when they are both present

This exercise will use the knowledge of inheritance you have gained so far to learn about the effects of **codominance**. You will then be able to produce a sentence about codominance towards the end of the exercise.

The three available alleles for blood groups are A, B and O.

11 a Write down which of these alleles are dominant in the space below.

....

b The codominance of these alleles will produce a fourth phenotype for blood group. Complete the table to show what this phenotype will be.

Alleles	Phenotype
AA or AO	blood group ....
BB or BO	blood group ....
....	blood group O
AB	blood group ....

c Circle all of the genotypes that are homozygous in the table.

LANGUAGE FOCUS

Sometimes we need to talk about how *probable* something is. We can use verbs and expressions of probability to help us. Some of these are:

unlikely to	*could be*	*likely to*	*should*
= improbable	50/50 possible	probable	almost certain

Examples:

• Recessive alleles are *unlikely* to be expressed in the phenotype.

• Heterozygous alleles *could be* expressed.

• A dominant allele would *be likely* to be expressed in the phenotype.

• Homozygous dominant alleles *should* be expressed in the next generation.

---

12 Your task is to produce a Punnett square to investigate the different combinations of blood groups that an offspring may express.

a Complete the Punnett square to show the offspring that could be produced for parents with the genotypes AA and BO.

		mother	
		B	O
father	A		
	A		

b For the Punnett Square above, circle the correct option to show what is likely to happen.

The blood group AB **could / should** be expressed in the phenotype of the offspring.

The blood group A **could / is unlikely** to be expressed in the phenotype of the offspring.

The blood group B is **will not / will** be expressed in the phenotype of the offspring.

c Write a sentence that explains the probability of the offspring having the blood group AB. You should use the following key words in your sentence:

codominant   phenotype

....

....

....

Chapter 17

Variation and selection

Science skills:

- become familiar with some of the key words related to variation and natural selection

- identify and explain some adaptive features that help an organism to survive

- learn about Darwin and his theory of evolution.

English skills:

- use linkers and the simple past tense in sentences about natural selection.

Exercise 17.1 Key words of variation

IN THIS EXERCISE YOU WILL:

Science skills:

- become familiar with the key words of variation and natural selection.

English skills:

- construct sentences using the simple past tense.

KEY WORDS

natural selection: a process in which individuals with advantageous features are more likely to survive, reproduce and pass on their alleles to the next generation

variation: differences between the individuals of the same species

The more that you identify and use the key words in each topic, the easier it becomes. This exercise is an opportunity to get used to using the key words related to **variation**.

1   An anagram is a puzzle where a word's letters have been reordered. To solve an anagram, you need to reorder the letters to make a real word. An example would be:

aniavitro is an anagram of *variation*

Solve the following anagrams to find key words related to variation and selection. Clues have been provided in brackets. The first has been done for you.

cidinonuousts (with intervals) .... *discontinuous* ....

a   cousinunto (without intervals) ....

b   aitmount (a change in DNA) ....

c   aitpaved (change to suit the environment) ....

d   exerthypo (cactus is an example) ....

e   hydetrophy (grows in water) ....

f   ceiltones (the survival of individuals due to their specific characteristics)

    ....

2   The history of evolution and **natural selection** has been developed by many different scientists throughout the years. Each scientist had their own beliefs and theories based on the evidence they could see at the time. These theories are used to explain the patterns of variation observed between generations.

LANGUAGE FOCUS

To talk about famous scientists and their theories, you generally need to use the past tense known as the simple past form. Most verbs in English are regular, which means that you make their affirmative past form by adding -*ed* (or -*d* if they end in -*e*) to the basic verb. For example:

*   suggest = suggested

*   propose = proposed

*   believe = believed

*   disprove = disproved

*   discover = discovered

Linnaeus *proposed* the modern classification system.

Charles Darwin *believed* that species evolved over time.

A few common verbs are irregular. If you use them often, you will remember them:

be – was/were;   think – thought;   write – wrote:

Charles Darwin *thought* that species evolved over time. He *wrote* about his beliefs in his many books.

Research what the following scientists' main ideas and beliefs were. Then use a suitable simple past form from below to write sentences about each scientist and their ideas / theories / beliefs.

believed   confirmed   discovered   disproved

proposed   proved   published   suggested

a   Thomas Hunt Morgan / Mendelian laws of inheritance

....

b   Jean-Baptiste Lamarck / spontaneous generation

....

c   Alfred Russel Wallace / theory of evolution

....

d   Charles Darwin / *On the Origin of Species*

....

e   Gregor Mendel / laws of genetic inheritance

....

Exercise 17.2 Darwin and evolution

IN THIS EXERCISE YOU WILL:

Science skills:

- learn about how Darwin proposed his theory of evolution.

English skills:

- use sentence linkers to describe the adaptive features of different animals.

KEY WORDS

adaptive feature: an inherited feature that helps an organism to survive and reproduce in its environment

Charles Darwin wrote a book called *On the Origin of Species*, which contained his theory of evolution. The way we think today is based on his theory – and the book came out in 1859!

3 Read the following text about Darwin and his theories. Then use the information to complete the table.

> Darwin proposed that there was some variation within a species that would allow it to better adapt to its environment. Darwin also noted that only the organisms that were well adapted to their environment would survive. This theory is commonly known as survival of the fittest.
>
> Darwin suggested that organisms with **adaptive features** would pass on their characteristics to their offspring and were more likely to reproduce than those that are not well adapted. This means that those organisms that are not well adapted will decrease in the population and the remaining population would be stronger and better as a whole.

Key word / term	Definition
	a system of ideas and principles used to explain something
	adjust to new conditions
	a particular feature of a thing or an organism
variation	
environment	

4 Look at Figure 17.1 and answer the following questions.

Figure 17.1: Two varieties of peppered moths.

The two moths in Figure 17.1 both live in an area where the trees are a dark colour as a result of pollution at a nearby factory. The number of moths was recorded over a period of time, and it was noted that the population of some of the moths decreased.

a The population of which type of moth decreased? ....

b Why did the population of this type of moth decrease?

....

....

c   Why were the trees a dark colour?

....

....

LANGUAGE FOCUS

There are different words that you can use when writing about the reason or purpose of something, and you want to link your observations (the *fact*) to the explanations (the *reason* or *purpose*):

Observation		**Explanation**
The tiger can catch its prey easily	*because / as*	it has very strong legs.

(*Because* and *as* here tell us the *reason*.)

The tiger has very strong legs	*so that*	it can catch its prey easily.

(*So that* and *in order that* refer to the *purpose*.)

---

5   Use the sentence linkers to write sentences about the adaptive features of animals.

as   because   so that

a   a bird's long, thin beak

....

b   the white fur of a polar bear

....

c   the long neck of a giraffe

....

d   the light bones of flying birds

....

Exercise 17.3 Adaptation of a lion

IN THIS EXERCISE YOU WILL:

Science skills:

• identify adaptive features from an image.

English skills:

• write a paragraph about the adaptation of the lion.

Lions are well adapted for survival in their environment. They are predators and use all of their physical characteristics to hunt and kill.

6 Look at Figure 17.2.

Figure 17.2: Lions in their environment.

a Label the image with at least two of the characteristics that the lion has in order to survive.

b Write a paragraph about how the lion is adapted to its environment. Refer to the features that you labelled in part a and write about them as complete sentences. Use *because*, *as* and *so that* to help you explain the adaptive features of the lion and link your observations to explanations.

....

....

....

....

....

....

....

....

....

c Explain what would happen to the lion population if they did not have the features you have written about. Your explanation should also link to the specific features.

....

....

....

....

> **LANGUAGE TIP**
>
> When you make a generalisation and talk about, for example, all lions, you can use *The lion...* or *Lions...* Remember not to use *The* with the plural when you want to generalise.

> Chapter 18

Organisms and their environment

Exercise 18.1 Ecological key terms

This exercise introduces you to key terms associated with ecology and their definitions.

1   Find the key terms for this topic in this word string and write them in the space below. There are nine to find.

environmentecologyhabitatpopulationcommunityecosystemenergyfoodchainfoodweb

....

....

....

2   Match the terms in question **1** with their definitions and write them in the correct place in the table.

Word	Definition
	the area where an organism lives
	the number of organisms of the same species living together in the same area at the same time
	a network of food chains connected together to show the flow of energy in that ecosystem
	shows the flow of energy from one organism to the next
	the study of organisms and their environment
	all of the organisms of different species that occupy the same habitat
	this is required for organisms to grow healthily
	an area that contains all of the organisms and their environment
	the surroundings of an organism

Exercise 18.2 Food chains and food webs

IN THIS EXERCISE YOU WILL:

Science skills:

- explain what happens as energy moves along a food chain.

English skills:

- use conditionals to hypothesise about the possible effects of changes in populations.

KEY WORDS

consumer: an organism that gets its energy by feeding on other organisms

food chain: a diagram showing the flow of energy from one organism to the next, beginning with a producer

food web: a network of interconnected food chains

producer: an organism that makes its own organic nutrients, generally using energy from sunlight, through photosynthesis

The aim of this exercise is to support your understanding of the energy changes in a food chain.

3 Read the information about **food chains** then write the terms in the word list into the boxes above the images.

> Energy from the Sun is passed along a food chain as animals consume other organisms. The food chain shows how the energy is passed from one level to another.
>
> A food chain shows the flow of energy between organisms. They usually begin with a plant called a **producer**. Animals follow next in the food chain and they are the **consumers**.

primary consumer   secondary consumer   producer

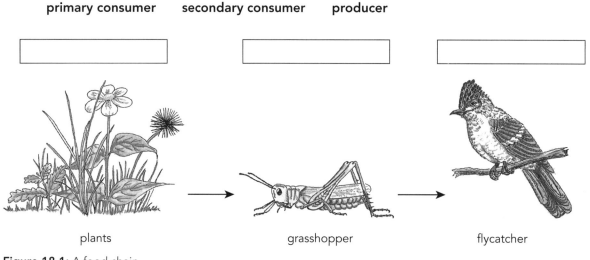

plants   grasshopper   flycatcher

Figure 18.1: A food chain.

4 Use the information from the previous question to complete the following paragraph.

The .... is the producer in this food chain. The producer gets their

energy from the .... before it is passed along the food chain. The plants

are eaten by the .... consumer, which in this case is the ....

The flycatcher is the secondary .... and gets its energy by eating

the grasshopper.

5   Food chains are generally short, as the organisms lose energy during respiration and other reactions. Some of the energy is 'lost' to the atmosphere and is considered to be wasted. Food chains can be linked together to form **food webs**. Look at the food web in Figure 18.2 and answer the questions that follow.

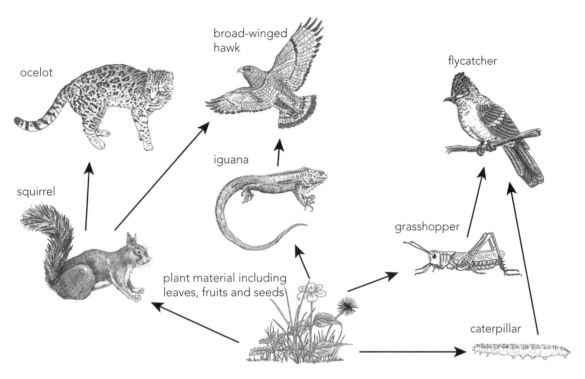

Figure 18.2: A food web.

a   How many producers are in this food web? ....

b   How many primary consumers are in this food web? ....

c   Name all of the primary consumers that you have counted.

    ....

d   What level of consumer is the ocelot? ....

LANGUAGE FOCUS

In science and other subjects, when we suggest an *imagined* situation, and the possible result in the present or future, then we are *hypothesising*. A useful structure for hypothesising is the *second conditional*:

If (subject) + past simple, (subject) *would* + infinitive

OR

(subject) *would* + infinitive *if* (subject) + past simple:

If the number of grasshoppers decreased, the flycatcher *would* struggle to survive.

The flycatcher *would* struggle to survive *if* the number of grasshoppers decreased.

When the sentence begins with *If*, we often add *then* in the middle:

If the number of grasshoppers decreased, *then* the flycatcher *would* struggle to survive.

The past simple form of regular verbs ends with *-ed*. For irregular verbs, it is the second form, for example:

eat, ate, eaten   give, gave, given   come, came, come   grow, grew, grown

---

6   Read the following text, and then answer the questions in the second conditional.

> If an organism within a food web suddenly increased or decreased in number, then this would have an effect on the other organisms in the food web. For example, if the number of grasshoppers dramatically decreased, then the flycatcher would struggle to get enough energy and may decrease in number. Similarly, the number of caterpillars may decrease because the flycatcher would have to consume more of them to survive.

Imagine that all of the iguanas suddenly increased, died or moved away from the ecosystem shown in Figure 18.2. What would happen? Complete the second conditional sentences to show what effect this would have on the other organisms in the food web.

a   If the population of iguanas increased, then the population of broad-winged

hawks would ....

b   If the population of iguanas decreased, then the population of plants

....

c   .... of iguanas decreased, then the

.... of grasshoppers ....

d Write your own full sentence using the second conditional to describe the effect of a change in the ocelot population on the population of squirrels.

....

....

Exercise 18.3 The human population

IN THIS EXERCISE YOU WILL:

Science skills:

- discuss how and why human populations are increasing rapidly.

English skills:

- use the appropriate language to describe increases and decreases in populations.

The population of the world has recently increased to over 7 billion people. This is due to people living longer, and the rising number of babies being born. This has been possible because of improvements in diet, farming and medicine. Unfortunately, this is having an effect on the environment as resources are needed to feed and shelter so many people. This exercise looks at the impacts of a rapidly increasing human population.

LANGUAGE FOCUS

When we need to talk about numbers going up or going down, we can use particular words and phrases to help us. For example:

go down – decrease, drop, fall:

The number of orangutans is *decreasing*.

The number of orangutans is *falling*.

go up – increase, rise, (climb):

The number of humans on earth is *increasing*.

The number of humans on earth is *rising*.

We can also use adverbs and adverbial phrases to express the speed of the increase or decrease.

For example:

slowly   gradually   at a steady rate   rapidly

slow ———————————————————————————▶ fast

7   The increase in human population has led to an increase in pollution. Air and water are becoming more polluted, and habitats and species are being threatened and in extreme cases can become extinct. This is due to the demands of the increasing population, as they require more food and shelter.

Complete the following sentences using the options available to get an overview of the effect of the increasing human population.

Increasing population means increasing use of cars, increasing planes, and increasing amounts of fuels being burnt. The gases produced in **burning / freezing** fossil fuels are being released into the atmosphere. This is contributing to the **decrease / increase** in air pollution. Rivers and lakes are being polluted by toxic chemicals, pesticides and oil spills. The **decreased / increased** demand for farming and the space needed for homes and factories are destroying habitats and the **people / species** that live within those habitats.

8   Look at Figure 18.3 and how the human population has changed in the past 2000 years.

LANGUAGE TIP

When you see passive structures in science texts, notice the tense of *to be*. It tells you about when the event or action is happening. For example:

The gases produced *are being* released into the atmosphere (*are being* is present continuous, so this is happening now).

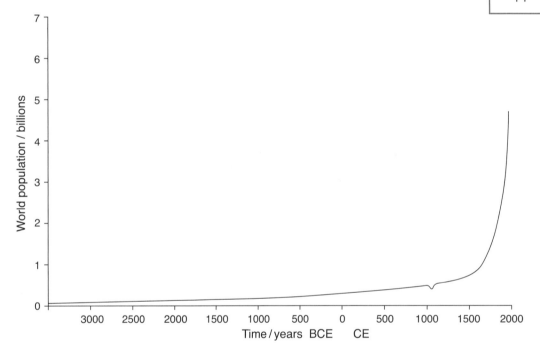

Figure 18.3: Change in human population since 3500 BCE.

Describe what happens to the population in the following time periods. Use the following words to describe the trends in the graph. One has already been done for you.

at a faster rate   at a slower rate   at a steady rate

decreasing   increasing   rapidly

Between the years 0 and 500 CE

the population is increasing at a steady rate

a   Between the years 500 and 1500 CE

....

b   Between the years 1500 and 2000 CE

....

9   Read the following paragraph and underline the three most important statements. Write the three statements in the space below to form a summary of the paragraph. For each statement, you should reword the sentence to be shorter and more concise.

> The human population has increased to over 7 billion people in recent years and most of this growth has taken place during the past 200–300 years. The death rate has been decreasing during this time, as there is less disease killing large numbers of people. This has been due to the advancement of modern medicine and the training of doctors and nurses. People have been getting immunised – which protects against disease – and so fewer people die from diseases that would have killed years before. The quality and quantity of food have improved too, as farming methods are able to produce large quantities of food at a lower cost. The diets of people have also improved and this is contributing to people living much longer. It was not that long ago when people would expect to live to their thirties or forties but now some people live well past 100 years old!

....

....

....

....

....

....

Chapter 19

Human influences on ecosystems

IN THIS CHAPTER YOU WILL:

Science skills:

- outline human impacts on ecosystems and how these can be reduced.

English skills:

- use linkers to describe causes and effects of global warming and climate change

- use conditional sentences to link action and consequence and to make predictions for sustainability measures

- use plurals in sentences about endangered species.

Exercise 19.1 Habitat destruction

IN THIS EXERCISE YOU WILL:

Science skills:

- outline how habitats are destroyed by humans.

English skills:

- use conditional sentences to talk about scientific facts and predictions.

Talking about the impact of humans on habitats requires conditional sentences to link the actions of humans with the consequences. This exercise will help you to write conditional sentences to link the action and consequence together.

1   Find the six words given in the word list in the puzzle below.

biodiversity   **breeding**   **captive**   **endangered**

extinction   **monoculture**

M	U	O	Q	C	Y	R	W	Y	N	Q	H	I	N	G
O	N	O	I	T	C	N	I	T	X	E	B	Z	N	W
N	D	C	H	Q	X	I	V	N	D	I	G	I	Q	D
O	N	E	E	M	A	F	L	H	O	Z	D	O	B	P
C	E	X	R	F	W	F	J	D	J	E	S	K	W	J
U	K	C	Z	E	C	Q	I	M	E	H	I	T	H	P
L	V	Z	W	M	G	V	W	R	H	K	H	X	F	R
T	W	J	O	P	E	N	B	P	S	R	G	C	E	U
U	I	B	D	R	W	U	A	A	W	O	N	E	I	U
R	B	Y	S	N	A	W	D	D	Y	X	H	V	Q	J
E	U	I	P	I	K	N	P	F	N	H	C	I	M	C
D	T	Y	M	R	A	M	W	K	I	E	U	T	X	D
Y	U	K	B	U	X	M	L	F	B	X	N	P	Z	B
V	K	M	P	W	T	A	P	W	L	D	Y	A	U	Z
Z	I	G	L	O	O	J	B	Y	X	B	H	C	L	C

LANGUAGE FOCUS

Sometimes we use *If…* at the start of sentences about scientific facts and known truths. When we do, we use the zero conditional. We form the zero conditional like this:

If the ice at the Poles *melts*, the sea level *rises*.

Coasts change shape if the sea level rises.

If goes in front of the condition needed (for example, *ice melts*), and both verbs in the sentence are written in the present form, to show that the consequence is always an effect of the condition.

ice at the Poles melts → sea level rises

= If the ice at the Poles *melts*, the sea level *rises*.

In science, we can also use the zero conditional to describe the effect of an action in an experiment:

If you *heat* the solution, the temperature *increases*.

NOTE: The zero conditional expresses something that is a fact, always true. The first conditional (Chapter 8) expresses a prediction:

Coasts *change if* the sea level *rises*. (fact – zero conditional)

If sea levels *rise* dramatically, many countries *will be* affected. (prediction about the future – first conditional)

2 Read the statement below, then write sentences using the zero conditional to show the consequences of the actions given. The first one has been done for you.

Humans destroy habitats when they use land to grow crops, farm live produce and build houses, factories and roads.

Action: Humans using too many fertilisers close to waterways.

Consequence: ....*If humans use too many fertilisers close to waterways, it leads to eutrophication.*...............................

    a Action: Humans adding pollutants to water.

      Consequence: ....

      ....

    b Action: Mining that destroys the soil and vegetation of a habitat.

      Consequence: ....

      ....

    c Action: Humans removing live corals from coral reefs.

      Consequence: ....

      ....

    d Action: Humans cutting down trees to make more paper.

      Consequence: ....

      ....

3 The loss of habitats is a great threat to biodiversity. Write a prediction using a first conditional sentence for each of the following sustainability measures. The first one has been done for you.

Only cutting down a few trees in one area.

If you only cut down a few trees, you will have more trees available.

    a Only cutting trees down to 1 m tall (coppicing).

      ....

    b Replacing trees that are cut down with new ones (replanting).

      ....

    c Prevent trees being cut down by enforcing government regulations.

      ....

    d Cutting down fewer trees by improving education.

      ....

Exercise 19.2 Endangered species

IN THIS EXERCISE YOU WILL:

Science skills:

- discuss some endangered species.

English skills:

- using plurals in your writing.

KEY WORD

endangered: at serious risk of becoming extinct

LANGUAGE FOCUS

The letter *s* is very important in English. When it comes at the end of a word, it can change the meaning of that word in a number of ways. Let's review them.

Plurals

Most plurals are formed by adding *-s* or *-es* to the noun (see Chapter 15):

A safari park contains many tigers.

Verbs

The he/she/it form of the present simple tense adds an *-s* to the end of the verb:

In fact, a safari park helps protect many endangered species.

Possessives

Possession, where the 'owner' is a person or animal, is also expressed using an *s*:

Darwin's theory of evolution. (Singular noun + apostrophe (') + *s*)

Many scientists' theories. (Plural noun + *s* + apostrophe ('))

Its and it's

Both these forms exist but mean different things.

Its = a possessive adjective:

The meerkat depends on *its* family or 'mob' for survival.

It's = usually means it is, occasionally it has. The ' tells you that some letters have been cut:

Meerkats use a special sound to warn of danger. *It's* similar to a song.

In formal and scientific writing, however, use *it is*, not *it's*.

4   Read the pairs of sentences and identify the plural forms. Then decide whether the ' is needed or not and copy the correct sentence. For example:

The tigers run very fast.

The tiger's run very fast.

The tigers run very fast.

a   The South China tiger is one of the worlds most endangered animals.

The South China tiger is one of the world's most endangered animals.

....

b   Three species of tiger are already extinct.

Three species' of tiger are already extinct.

....

c   If tigers become extinct, it affects the ecosystem.

If tiger's become extinct, it affects the ecosystem.

....

d   Hunting by human's is one of the main dangers to tigers.

Hunting by humans is one of the main dangers to tigers.

....

5   The hawksbill sea turtle is an **endangered** species and lives in a warm water habitat. Its estimated that there are only 8000 turtles left on Earth. The hawksbill turtle uses its nest to lay up to 3000 eggs. The turtle likes to lay its nest in sandy seabeds. Coral reef sponges are the primary sources of food and the turtle has very little competition for this food. Sea turtles have existed on Earth longer than humans.

a   Find and copy the plurals in the text above.

....

b   One sentence includes an incorrect use of *its*. Find the sentence and rewrite correctly.

....

c   State what the two correct *its* refer to.

....

d   Research the hawksbill turtle and write your own sentences. Use plurals and possessive forms correctly.

....

....

....

Exercise 19.3 Climate change

IN THIS EXERCISE YOU WILL:

Science skills:

- describe the causes and effects of climate change.

English skills:

- use linkers to describe causes and effects.

6   a   Read the paragraph and underline the causes of climate change and circle the effects of climate change. Then use the causes and effects to complete the table that follows.

Climate change is caused by greenhouse gases such as carbon dioxide and methane. Carbon dioxide is released during the combustion of fossil fuels and methane is released by cattle and the anaerobic decomposition of plant matter. The greenhouse gases trap heat energy within the atmosphere and this increases the overall temperature of the Earth. This change in temperature causes weather patterns to change and events such as flooding and hurricanes occur more frequently. The polar ice caps melt and this increases sea levels.

Causes of climate change	Effects of climate change
carbon dioxide released into atmosphere	weather patterns change

LANGUAGE FOCUS

To link a cause and an effect, we use linkers such as *due to, owing to, because of* and *(be) caused by*. All four are followed by a noun phrase or by *-ing*:

Weather patterns are changing *due to* greenhouse gases being released and trapped.

Owing to hunting for food and sport, many species are in danger of extinction.

Scientists are concerned about the future *because of* greenhouses gases.

Climate change is likely to *be caused by* the human impact on the environment.

b   Use your answers in the table in question **6a** to write four sentences that link the causes and effects of climate change. Use the linkers in the Language Focus box.

....

....

....

....

c   Read the notes below then write three sentences explaining the effects of greenhouse gases. Use the information in the notes and your own ideas. Remember to use the linkers in the Language Focus box.

The effects of climate change are:

- Extreme climates – hurricanes, heavy rainfall → flooding.

- Water evaporates from fertile areas to form deserts.

- Polar caps melt which lead to rising sea levels and flooding.

....

....

....

....

....

Exercise 19.4 Limiting the effects of climate change

IN THIS EXERCISE YOU WILL:

Science skills:

* consider ways of reducing the effects of climate change.

English skills:

* use the second conditional form.

This exercise looks at ideas for limiting climate change and the possible effects these could have.

LANGUAGE FOCUS

You have already seen how to use *If* to talk about facts and predictions. You can also use it to express *hypothetical situations*, that is to speculate about situations that might not happen:

If all the trees in the Amazon *were* cut down, it *would be* a disaster for our planet.

As you can see from the example, to do this you use *If* with the past tense and *would* + verb. You can also use *might* to express possibility:

If all the trees in the Amazon *were* cut down, we *might* find another way to make oxygen.

The *If* can also go in the middle of the sentence:

It *would be* a disaster for our planet *if* all the trees in the Amazon *were* cut down.

This structure is called the second conditional. It is different from the first conditional in meaning because the first conditional is something we think is possible:

If it rains all month, the rivers *will* flood.

If it rained for a year, many farmers *would* lose all their animals and plants.

Read the text and look at Figure 19.1 and then use the second conditional to complete the task below.

Climate change is caused by greenhouse gases (carbon dioxide, methane, chlorofluorocarbons (CFCs)) which trap heat energy in the Earth's atmosphere. The heat energy cannot radiate out of the atmosphere as it should do.

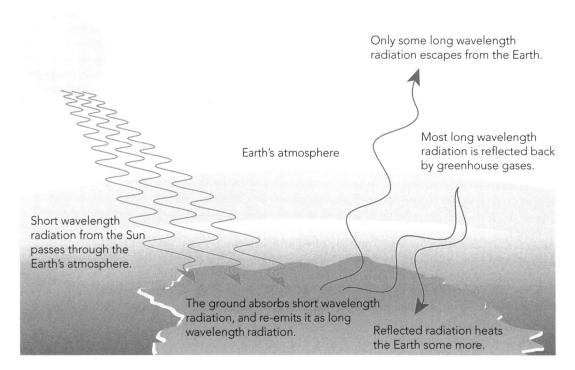

Only some long wavelength radiation escapes from the Earth.

Earth's atmosphere

Most long wavelength radiation is reflected back by greenhouse gases.

Short wavelength radiation from the Sun passes through the Earth's atmosphere.

The ground absorbs short wavelength radiation, and re-emits it as long wavelength radiation.

Reflected radiation heats the Earth some more.

Figure 19.1: Effect of greenhouse gases on Earth.

Many people and governments are campaigning to fight climate change and have come up with the following ideas to limit the effects of climate change:

- burn fewer fossil fuels

- cut down fewer forests and trees (which take in carbon dioxide from the atmosphere)

- replant forests that have been cut down previously

- stop using CFCs (found in aerosols and refrigerators)

- collect methane from landfill sites.

7   Choose two of the ideas for limiting climate change and speculate about what effects they would or might have, using the second conditional. An example has been done for you.

    If fewer trees and forests were cut down, it would reduce deforestation.

    ....

    ....

    ....

    ....

Chapter 20

Biotechnology and genetic modification

IN THIS CHAPTER YOU WILL:

Science skills:

- identify biotechnology key words from their definitions
- understand how pectinase is used in fruit juice production
- outline how insulin is produced using recombinant DNA.

English skills:

- use articles, passive sentences and prepositions correctly.

Exercise 20.1 Key words

IN THIS EXERCISE YOU WILL:

Science skills:

- learn about key words associated with biotechnology.

English skills:

- use articles correctly in a sentence.

KEY WORDS

biofuel: a fuel that is made by mixing ethanol (made by the anaerobic respiration of yeast) with petrol

genetic modification: changing the genetic material of an organism by removing, changing or inserting individual genes

pectinase: an enzyme that is used to digest pectin, increasing the quantity of juice that can be extracted from fruit, and clarifying the juice

recombinant plasmid: a small circle of DNA, found in bacteria, which contains both the bacterial DNA and DNA from a different organism

In this exercise you will identify biotechnology key terms from their definitions and then use those key terms to construct a word search.

1   For the following definitions, write the appropriate key word.

   a   a small circle of DNA, found in bacteria, which contains both the bacterial
       DNA and DNA from a different organism ....

   b   enzymes (biological catalysts) that cut DNA at specific points, and leave a
       short length of unpaired bases at each end ....

   c   using organisms, usually microorganisms, to produce required substances
       ....

   d   an enzyme that is used to digest pectin, increasing the quantity of juice that
       can be extracted from fruit, and clarifying the juice ....

   e   a fuel that is made by mixing ethanol (made by the anaerobic respiration of
       yeast) with petrol...

   f   a vessel, usually made of steel or glass, in which microorganisms can be
       grown to produce a required product ....

   g   an enzyme that joins two DNA molecules together ....

2   Write your answers to question 1 in the blank word search grid below. You can
    write them horizontally, vertically or diagonally. Fill in the remaining boxes with
    other letters to make your word search. Then give your word search to a friend to
    see if they can find the correct key words.

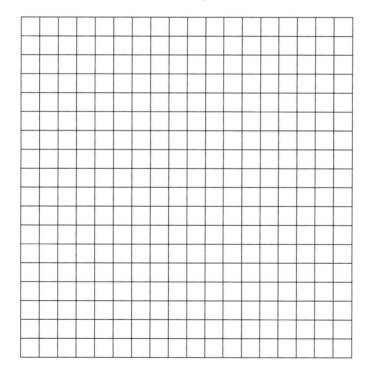

LANGUAGE FOCUS

Using *a* or *an*

The choice of *a* or *an* depends on the first sound in the word (noun or adjective) that follows it.

If the next word begins with a consonant <u>sound</u>, use *a*. For example:

A digital meter; *a* numerical value; *a* universal law.

If the next word begins with a vowel <u>sound</u> (*a, e, i, o, u*), use *an*. For example:

An analogue meter; *an* hour; *an* endangered species.

You use *a* or *an* when you are talking about something for the first time, or if you are not talking about a specific thing. After the first time you refer to something in a text, you use the article *the* – the reader knows what thing you are talking about. For example:

This exercise looks at *an* enzyme. (Which enzyme? The reader doesn't know yet.)

The enzyme helps clarify juice. (This is specifically the enzyme that you mentioned in the previous sentence.)

3   Complete the sentences with *a*, *an* or *the*.

   a   **Pectinase** is .... enzyme used to digest pectin.

   b   **Biofuel** is .... fuel that mixes ethanol with petrol.

   c   Sticky ends join together the ends of .... DNA molecule.

   d   A **recombinant plasmid** is .... small circle of DNA. ....
       recombinant plasmid contains DNA for different organisms.

   e   **Genetic modification** changes the genetic material of .... organism.
       .... modification involves the removal or insertion of genes.

Exercise 20.2 Pectinase in fruit juice production

IN THIS EXERCISE YOU WILL:

Science skills:

- understand the role of pectinase in fruit juice production.

English skills:

- construct passive sentences in a laboratory method.

Pectinase breaks down pectin, and when broken down it is easier to squeeze juice from fruits like apples and oranges. Adding pectinase to cloudy fruit juice helps to make it clear so the juice looks more attractive and refreshing.

LANGUAGE FOCUS

When you give instructions for a procedure or experiment, you tell someone what to do, so instructions are written using the form of the verb known as the imperative. The imperative is simple to make, as it is the basic form of the verb. For example, *to look, to observe*:

Look at the juice. *Observe* the changes.

In a sequence of instructions, sequencers are often used to emphasise the order of the steps.

First, look at the juice. *Then* observe the changes. *Finally*, compare with beaker B.

However, when you write a report on the procedure or experiment, you need to write what you did. An appropriate form to use is the *passive*. Scientists often use the passive voice because what is happening is more important than who is performing the action. Remember the three simple steps for turning an instruction into a passive sentence.

Here is an instruction: *Record the volume of pectinase.*

To make this instruction passive:

1   Find the object of the sentence. The object is the 'thing' that the verb is acting on: *the volume of pectinase*. This becomes the subject of the new sentence.

2   Then add *was* or *were*. Use *was* if the object is singular and *were* if it is plural. So in this case: *was*.

3   Next, use the past participle of the verb. Remember that for regular verbs, you make the past participle by adding *-ed*. For irregular verbs, you can find three forms in a dictionary or verb table: the past participle is the third form. For example: take/took/*taken*. *Record* is regular; the past participle is *recorded*.

This gives you the passive sentence:

The volume of pectinase *was recorded*.

When you have your passive sentences, you can add sequencers like *Firstly, After that, Next*, and so on. This will give you a clear report.

4 The effect of pectinase on orange pulp can be observed in the laboratory using the following method.

- Chop the orange into small pieces. These should be no larger than 5 mm³.
- Divide the 100 g of orange into two separate beakers.
- Add 2 ml of pectinase to one of the beakers and stir with the glass rod.
- Add 2 ml of water to the second beaker of orange and stir with the glass rod.
- Cover the beakers with plastic wrap and incubate at 40 °C for 20 minutes.
- Line the funnels with the filter paper.
- Place the funnel over the measuring cylinder and add the pulp from each beaker.
- Record the volume of juice obtained from each sample of orange pulp every five minutes until the juice no longer filters through the paper.

Rewrite the method as a report, using the passive and sequencers. The first sentence has been done for you.

Chop the orange into small pieces no larger than 5 mm³.

First, the orange was chopped into small pieces no larger than 5 mm³.

a Divide the 100 g of orange into two beakers.

....

b Add 2 ml of pectinase to beaker A.

....

c Add 2 ml of water to beaker B.

....

d Stir both beakers with a glass rod.

....

e Cover the beakers with plastic wrap.

....

f Incubate the beakers at 40 °C for 20 minutes.

....

g Line two funnels with the filter paper.

....

h Place each funnel over a measuring cylinder and add the pulp from each beaker.

....

i Record the volume of juice obtained from each sample of orange pulp every five minutes.

....

Exercise 20.3 Genetic modification

IN THIS EXERCISE YOU WILL:

Science skills:

- outline how human insulin is produced by genetic modification.

English skills:

- use prepositions in a simple method.

KEY WORDS

DNA ligase: an enzyme that joins two DNA molecules together

insulin: a hormone secreted by the pancreas, which decreases blood glucose concentration

restriction enzymes: enzymes (biological catalysts) that cut DNA at specific points, and leave a short length of unpaired bases at each end

Insulin is a hormone, produced by the pancreas, that allows your body to use glucose for energy. When a person has diabetes, their body either doesn't make enough insulin or can't effectively use the insulin it does make. In this exercise you will learn how human insulin can be produced by genetic modification.

LANGUAGE FOCUS

Prepositions are important when constructing sentences. Prepositions include *in, on, from, by, behind, for, at* and so on. A preposition sits before a noun and shows the noun's relationship to the words in front of the preposition. In science we often use relationships of place and time in order to talk about the position and movement of things.

There are many uses of prepositions. However, there are not really any rules for them and they do not translate easily from language to language. Therefore, the best way to learn them is as part of phrases or sentences. This is why they appear more than once in this book, so that you can become familiar with seeing and using them.

Common examples from biology include:

We measure the length *of* insulin cells *in* micrometres. (the length *of*... / to measure something *in*...)

In red blood cells, oxygen molecules bind *with* haemoglobin. (*in* cells / bind *with*...)

5 **a** Read this paragraph and circle the correct prepositions.

Insulin is produced **at / on** an industrial scale because it is easy and cheap, and a lot can be made **in / on** a short space **for / of** time. Scientists use restriction enzymes and DNA ligase to carry out the following in order to make insulin available **by / for** humans.

b Complete the method with suitable prepositions.

  i Restriction enzymes cut the gene .... DNA.

  ii Plasmid is removed .... a bacterium.

  iii **Restriction enzymes** are used to cut the plasmid open.

   Insulin gene is inserted .... the plasmid and sealed .... **DNA ligase**.

  iv Plasmid is placed .... a bacterium to form recombinant DNA.

  v Bacteria multiply rapidly .... a fermenter to produce large amounts of insulin quickly and cheaply.

c Referring to the method in part b, answer the questions.

  i Which molecule acts as a 'pair of scissors'?

   ....

  ii Identify the molecule that acts as a 'glue' to join the two pieces of DNA.

   ....

  iii Explain why making insulin in this way is beneficial.

   ....

> Glossary

Command Words

Below are the Cambridge International definitions for command words which may be used in exams. The information in this section is taken from the Cambridge IGCSE™ Biology syllabus (0610/0970) for examination from 2023. You should always refer to the appropriate syllabus document for the year of your examination to confirm the details and for more information. The syllabus document is available on the Cambridge International website www.cambridgeinternational.org.

calculate: work out from given facts, figures or information

compare: identify/comment on similarities and/or differences

define: give precise meaning

describe: state the points of a topic / give characteristics and main features

determine: establish an answer using the information available

evaluate: judge or calculate the quality, importance, amount, or value of something

explain: set out purposes or reasons / make the relationships between things evident / provide why and/or how and support with relevant evidence

give: produce an answer from a given source or recall/memory

identify: name/select/recognise

outline: set out main points

predict: suggest what may happen based on available information

sketch: make a simple freehand drawing showing the key features, taking care over proportions

state: express in clear terms

suggest: apply knowledge and understanding to situations where there are a range of valid responses in order to make proposals / put forward considerations

Key Words

absorption: the movement of nutrients from the alimentary canal into the blood

active immunity: long-term defence against a pathogen by antibody production in the body

active transport: the movement of molecules or ions through a cell membrane from a region of lower concentration to a region of higher concentration (i.e. against a concentration gradient) using energy from respiration

adaptive feature: an inherited feature that helps an organism to survive and reproduce in its environment

adrenaline: a hormone secreted by the adrenal glands, which prepares the body for fight or flight

aerobic respiration: chemical reactions that take place in mitochondria, which use oxygen to break down glucose and other nutrient molecules to release energy for the cell to use

alimentary canal: the part of the digestive system through which food passes as it moves from the mouth to the anus

alleles: alternative forms of a gene

alveoli (singular: alveolus): tiny air-filled sacs in the lungs where gas exchange takes place

anaerobic respiration: chemical reactions in cells that break down nutrient molecules to release energy, without using oxygen

antibiotic: a substance that are taken into the body, and which kill bacteria but do not affect human cells or viruses

antibodies: molecules secreted by white blood cells, which bind to pathogens and help to destroy them

antigen: a chemical that is recognised by the body as being 'foreign' – that is, it is not part of the body's normal set of chemical substances – and stimulates the production of antibodies

artery: a thick-walled vessel that takes high-pressure blood away from the heart

asexual reproduction: a process resulting in the production of genetically identical offspring from one parent

balanced diet: a diet that contains all of the required nutrients, in suitable proportions, and the right amount of energy

Benedict's solution: a blue liquid that turns orange-red when heated with reducing sugar

binomial: an adjective for a name with two words

biofuel: a fuel that is made by mixing ethanol (made by the anaerobic respiration of yeast) with petrol

biuret reagent: a blue solution that turns purple when mixed with amino acids or proteins

bronchiole: a small tube that takes air from a bronchus to every part of the lungs

bronchus: one of the two tubes (plural: bronchi) that takes air from the trachea into the lungs

capillary: a tiny vessel with walls only one cell thick, that takes blood close to body cells

carbohydrates: substances that include sugars, starch and cellulose; they contain carbon, hydrogen and oxygen

catalyst: a substance that increases the rate of a chemical reaction and is not changed by the reaction

cell wall: a tough layer outside the cell membrane; found in the cells of plants, fungi and bacteria

characteristics: visible features of an organism

chromosome: a length of DNA, found in the nucleus of a cell; it contains genetic information in the form of many different genes

circulatory system: a system of blood vessels with a pump and valves to ensure one-way flow of blood

codominance: alleles that are both expressed in the phenotype when they are both present

concentration gradient: when the concentration of particles is different in one area than another

consumer: an organism that gets its energy by feeding on other organisms

coronary heart disease (CHD): disease caused by blockage of the coronary arteries

dichotomous key: a way of identifying an organism, by working through pairs of statements that lead you to its name

diffusion: the net movement of particles from a region of their higher concentration to a region of their lower concentration (i.e. down a concentration gradient), as a result of their random movement

digestion: the breakdown of food

DNA ligase: an enzyme that joins two DNA molecules together

dominant allele: an allele that is expressed if it is present (e.g. G)

embryo: the ball of cells that is produced by repeated division of the zygote

endangered: at serious risk of becoming extinct

enzymes: proteins that are involved in all metabolic reactions, where they function as biological catalysts

excretion: the removal of the waste products of metabolism and substances in excess of requirements

food chain: a diagram showing the flow of energy from one organism to the next, beginning with a producer

food web: a network of interconnected food chains

gene: a length of DNA that codes for one protein

genetic modification: changing the genetic material of an organism by removing, changing or inserting individual genes

genotype: the genetic makeup of an organism in terms of the alleles present (e.g. GG)

glucagon: a hormone secreted by the pancreas, which increases blood glucose concentration

glucose: a sugar that is used in respiration to release energy

heterozygous: having two different alleles of a particular gene (e.g. Gg)

homeostasis: the maintenance of a constant internal environment

homozygous: having two identical alleles of a particular gene (e.g. GG or gg)

hormones: chemicals that are produced by a gland and carried in the blood, which alter the activities of their specific target organs

implantation: attachment of the embryo to the lining of the uterus

insulin: a hormone secreted by the pancreas, which decreases blood glucose concentration

kinetic energy: energy of moving objects

lignin: a hard, strong, waterproof substance that forms the walls of xylem vessels

limiting factor: a factor that is in short supply, which stops an activity (such as photosynthesis) happening at a faster rate

meiosis: division of a diploid nucleus resulting in four genetically different haploid nuclei; this is sometimes called a reduction division

metabolism: the chemical reactions that take place in living organisms

mitochondria: small structures in a cell, where aerobic respiration releases energy from glucose

mitosis: division of a cell nucleus resulting in two genetically identical nuclei (i.e. with the same number and kind of chromosomes as the parent nucleus)

natural selection: a process in which individuals with advantageous features are more likely to survive, reproduce and pass on their alleles to the next generation

neurone: a cell that is specialised for conducting electrical impulses rapidly

nucleus: a structure containing DNA in the form of chromosomes

organ: a group of tissues that work together to perform a particular function

organ system: several organs that work together to perform a particular function

osmosis: the diffusion of water molecules through a partially permeable membrane

passive immunity: short-term defence against a pathogen by antibodies acquired from another individual, such as from mother to infant

pathogens: microorganisms that cause disease, such as bacteria

pectinase: an enzyme that is used to digest pectin, increasing the quantity of juice that can be extracted from fruit, and clarifying the juice

phenotype: the observable features of an organism

phloem: a plant tissue made up of living cells joined end to end; it transports substances made by the plant, such as sucrose and amino acids

photosynthesis: the process by which plants synthesise carbohydrates from raw materials using energy from light

pollination: the transfer of pollen grains from the male part of a plant (anther of stamen) to the female part of a plant (stigma)

producer: an organism that makes its own organic nutrients, generally using energy from sunlight, through photosynthesis

product: the new substance formed by a chemical reaction

puberty: the time at which sexual maturity is reached

recessive allele: an allele that is only expressed when there is no dominant allele of the gene present (e.g. g)

recombinant plasmid: a small circle of DNA, found in bacteria, which contains both the bacterial DNA and DNA from a different organism

reflex action: a means of automatically and rapidly integrating and coordinating stimuli with the responses of effectors

reflex arc: a series of neurones (sensory, relay and motor) that transmit electrical impulses from a receptor to an effector

respiration: the chemical reactions in cells that break down nutrient molecules and release energy for metabolism

restriction enzymes: enzymes (biological catalysts) that cut DNA at specific points, and leave a short length of unpaired bases at each end

sexual reproduction: a process involving the fusion of two gametes to form a zygote and the production of offspring that are genetically different from each other

specialised cell: a cell that is responsible for a particular function. An example of a specialised cell is a red blood cell. The function of a red blood cell is to carry oxygen around the body

stimulus (plural: stimuli): a change in the environment that can be detected by organisms

substrate: the substance that an enzyme causes to react

symptoms: features that you experience when you have a disease

tissue: a group of similar cells that work together to perform a particular function

transmissible disease: a disease that can be passed from one host to another; transmissible diseases are caused by pathogens

urea: a waste product produced in the liver, from the breakdown of excess amino acids

ureter: one of a pair of tubes that carries urine from the kidneys to the bladder

urethra: the tube that carries urine from the bladder to the outside

variation: differences between the individuals of the same species

vascular bundles: collections of xylem tubes and phloem vessels running side by side, which form the veins in a leaf

vasoconstriction: narrowing of arterioles, caused by the contraction of the muscle in their walls

vasodilation: widening of arterioles, caused by the relaxation of the muscle in their walls

vein: a thin-walled vessel that takes low-pressure blood back to the heart

vertebrate: an organism that has a backbone/spinal cord, such as mammals, amphibians, birds, reptiles and fish

xylem: a plant tissue made up of dead, empty cells joined end to end; it transports water and mineral ions and helps to support the plant

zygote: a cell that is formed by the fusion of two gametes